EDEXCEL

AS LEVEL
MUSIC
TECHNOLOGY

Revision
Guide

First published 2018 in Great Britain by
Rhinegold Education
14-15 Berners Street
London W1T 3LJ, UK
www.rhinegoldeducation.co.uk

© 2018 Rhinegold Education
a division of Music Sales Limited

You should always check the current
requirements of your examination,
since these may change.

Editor: Imogen Willis
Cover and book design: Fresh Lemon Australia

EDEXCEL AS Level Music Technology Revision Guide
Order No. RHG347
ISBN: 978-1-78558-633-0

Exclusive Distributors:
Music Sales Ltd
Distribution Centre, Newmarket Road
Bury St Edmunds, Suffolk IP33 3YB, UK

Printed in the EU

EDEXCEL

AS LEVEL MUSIC TECHNOLOGY

Revision Guide

JAMES REEVELL

Adapted from the previous
Edexcel AS Level Music Technology
Revision Guide, which was authored
by Chris Duffill and Jonny Martin

RHINEGOLD
EDUCATION

Contents

The author

James Reevell

is a teacher, author and examiner with extensive experience in delivering Music and Music Technology A Level courses. He studied Music at Durham University, completed a Masters at Manchester Metropolitan University, and has experience teaching in sixth form colleges across the north of England. James has worked as a Subject Leader for Visual and Creative Arts with responsibility for courses in Art, Dance, Drama, Music and Music Technology. He has contributed to study and revision guides for A Level Music, Music Technology and GCSE Music as both author and consultant. James delivers nationwide training to teachers with a particular focus on Music Technology and Popular Music.

Acknowledgements

The author would like to recognise the significant contributions of others to this book, in particular, Chris Duffill and Jonny Martin, whose previous work and research formed the basis for this updated edition for the 2017 specification. Thanks also go to Imogen Willis from Rhinegold Education for her support and guidance in putting this book together and to Phil Gambrill from Fresh Lemon Design for his patience and the extensive work he has put into the diagrams and page setting.

The course

Congratulations on choosing to study the Edexcel AS Level Music Technology course!

The course is challenging and exciting, designed to give you an in-depth range of knowledge and skills over a breadth of content to prepare you for both further study and work in the music technology industry. Your work on the course will develop your practical skills but also your ability to critically listen to, analyse and produce music.

In this guide you will find useful reminders about:

- How the paper is structured
- How many marks are in each section
- What information you need to know
- How the questions will be presented in the exam
- Strategies that will help you to achieve your best in the exams.

1. **Component 1**	Recording	**60 marks:** 20% of the total AS Level mark
2. **Component 2**	Technology-based composition	**60 marks:** 20% of the total AS Level mark
3. **Component 3**	Listening and analysing	**60 marks:** 25% of the total AS Level mark
4. **Component 4**	Producing and analysing	**84 marks:** 35% of the total AS Level mark

This book is designed to help you prepare for Components 3 and 4. You will be expected to apply the knowledge and skills you have developed whilst completing your recording and composition work in Components 1 and 2, along with your understanding of music technology theory.

Summary: The non-examined assessment tasks

Component 1 – Recording

- The recording is worth 60 marks, and 20% of your AS level
- You must adapt the length of the song so that it lasts between 2 and 2½ minutes. You should also adapt the instrumentation of the song to fit the requirements of the question paper and the resources available to you
- The final recording will be marked by an examiner; you will also submit a logbook
- There is no requirement to perform in the same style, key or arrangement as the original, but the exam board will give you a list of compulsory instruments you must record, and additional instruments of which you have a choice
- You are assessed on the quality of the recording, so the **capture**, editing and mixing and production are more important than the musical performance
- However, the quality of the musical performance can affect the outcome; an out-of-time guitar will be much more difficult to balance and blend and may take time and extra processing to fix.

Component 2 – Technology-based composition

- The composition is worth 60 marks, and 20% of your AS level
- You will be provided with two samples to use:

  a 10–15 second sample of a melody and/or harmony

  a 2–4 second sample of a vocal phrase, sound effect or percussion sound.

- Your composition must be 2½ minutes long
- It will be marked by an examiner; you will also submit a logbook
- You will demonstrate your understanding of melody, harmony, rhythm, texture, and form/structure through completion of a practical task
- You will be assessed on your use of **synthesis**, **sampling**, creative effects, your editing of the mix, the style/coherence of your track, and your response to the chosen brief, as well as the musical elements above.

The exams

Component 3

1 hour 15 minutes

Section A (44 marks)

- Three questions worth 10 marks each and one question worth 14 marks.

Section B (16 marks)

- One extended response question comparing the production features of two tracks worth 16 marks.

60 marks (25%)

What will the exam look like?

Section A questions

- Short answer questions related to four different songs
- These will be chosen by Edexcel and could be from any of the eras or styles listed in the exam specification
- Section 3 in this guide provides a brief overview of the key features associated with each style.

Section B questions

- One extended response question worth 16 marks that will ask you to compare the production techniques used in two different tracks
- The tracks will share some sort of connection; they might be cover versions, or songs by the same producer.

In the exam, you will have your own copy of the recordings, so you can move to the specific time references in the questions, or just replay a certain section if you need to listen to it again. Your school or college will provide you with a means of listening to the recordings in the exam. If you use a computer, you are not permitted to access any other software like **DAWs**, or use other equipment like **MIDI** keyboards.

Things to remember for Component 3:

- Because you have control of the music in the exam, you can easily focus on what you need to listen to, but be careful: don't spend too much time repeating the music for one question

- Keep an eye on the clock to make sure you are using your time effectively
- The extended response question is worth nearly 30% of the available marks; that relates to around 20 minutes of exam time
- Use appropriate music technology terminology in your answers.

Component 4

1 hour 45 minutes with 10 minutes setting up time

Section A (68 marks)

- Five questions related to audio and **MIDI** stems provided, including written questions and practical tasks
- You will produce three bounces of the practical tasks you have completed
- You will complete a guided mix of the parts to produce one further bounce.

Section B (16 marks)

- Extended response question evaluating a specific signal process, effect or music technology hardware unit.

84 marks (35%)

What will the exam look like?

Section A questions

- You will be guided through a variety of processes which require you to demonstrate both your practical and theoretical knowledge of music technology
- This will require you to problem-solve, think logically and find solutions as part of the tasks on the paper
- At the end of Section A, you will be provided with a number of tasks that you will complete to create an effective mix of the materials you have been given.

Section B question

- You will answer an extended response question that will focus on a specific signal process, effect or music technology hardware unit worth 16 marks
- You will be provided with a diagram, photograph or other stimulus; you will need to apply your knowledge of music technology to the scenario given in the question

- To achieve top marks, you will need to examine and dissect it, commenting on how it achieves (or does not achieve) its purpose, making judgements and drawing your own conclusions
- You will justify your answer using the knowledge and understanding you have built up whilst completing your coursework and study as part of the course.

You will have access to your own computer, **DAW**, **MIDI** keyboard and headphones. You will not be able to access anything else on the computer. You will be provided with your own copy of the stem files and an exam paper with instructions to tell you what you need to do. You will bounce your work during the course of the exam and at the end of the session, your bounces and paper will be submitted to Edexcel.

Things to remember for Component 4:

- Answer the questions in order on the paper; the processes completed in earlier questions might affect those later on
- Keep an eye on the clock to make sure that you are allocating enough time to the parts of the exam that are worth more marks
- Make sure you allow yourself enough time to mix down the tracks and complete your final bounce – this is worth just over 20% of the marks on the paper
- The extended written response question is worth just under 25% of the marks on the paper, so plan to spend around 25 minutes on it
- After you've done this, make sure you allow yourself enough time to check through your written work and your bounces at the end of the exam
- Include diagrams and graphs wherever you can in your answers; they help to get your answer across with detail and can score you plenty of credit, especially if you label them with units and other annotations
- If discussing controls on equipment, don't just reword the question; you won't get any credit if, for '*threshold*' you write '*the threshold changes the threshold*'
- In your bounces, be careful not to cut off the last note or the **reverb** tail
- Do not apply effects or processing that the paper does not require. Otherwise, you might mask what the examiner is listening for
- Careful with your output level – use the mixer faders to ensure that the track is sufficiently loud but not distorting
- The stem files are often mastered at varying volumes. Make sure that you listen to the overall mix and aim for loud drums with an audible kick and that you can hear all the words in the vocal part. Then gradually bring in the other tracks to produce an effective overall mix.

Principles and practice

Capture of sound

- A microphone is a **transducer**; a device that converts between different types of energy
- In this case, it is converting sound, and thus variations in air pressure into electrical energy
- The sensitive transducer element of a microphone is called its **capsule**
- Different types of microphone work in different ways; you need to know about dynamic and **condenser microphones**
- Dynamic microphones are sometimes known as moving coil microphones, and condensers are sometimes known as capacitor microphones.

Comparing dynamic and condenser microphones

Dynamic microphones	Condenser microphones
<ul><li>Generally inexpensive</li><li>Robust</li><li>Can withstand high SPL/volume</li><li>Resistant to moisture</li><li>Good for live use</li><li>Does not require **phantom power**</li><li>Limited HF response; suitable for bass instruments.</li></ul>	<ul><li>Sensitive, giving effective **capture** of quiet sounds</li><li>Flat and accurate **frequency** responses</li><li>Able to capture a wide frequency range</li><li>Generally able to capture a brighter signal than dynamic microphones and better for capture of high frequencies</li><li>Good **signal-to-noise ratio**; high output volume and thus low **noise**</li><li>Wide dynamic range</li><li>Suitable for most studio work.</li></ul>

Phantom power

- **Phantom power** is required to charge the capacitor of a **condenser microphone**
- Some condenser microphones can also be powered by a battery
- Many **mixing desks** and **audio interfaces** allow you to switch phantom power (48V) on and off; this is important as it can damage some equipment.

Polar patterns

- A microphone's polar pattern describes how it picks up sound from around the **capsule**

- One of the most useful polar patterns for close-mic recording is **cardioid** ('heart-shaped')

- Cardioid microphones reject sound from behind the microphone, and minimise the amount of **reverb** and/ or **noise** from behind the microphone that is **captured**

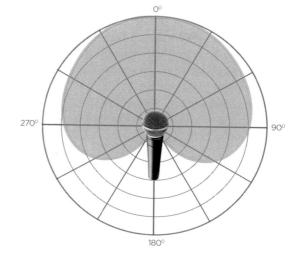

- Engineers can also avoid capturing unwanted background noise and **spill** by:
    - Ensuring performer(s) wear (closed-back) headphones
    - Keeping the monitor mix relatively quiet in headphones
    - Using acoustic screens/isolation booths
    - Making use of **overdubbing**.

Setting the gain

- When recording, you should carefully consider your gain structure
- This means that you will use the dynamic range of audio equipment to its best advantage in order to minimise noise and unwanted distortion
- To do this, it is necessary to set appropriate gain levels on each piece of equipment
- If the volume on an electric piano is set at a low level, and the audio interface gain is turned up to the maximum, you will capture lots of hiss
- If the volume on the electric piano is at its highest level, you risk capturing a distorted signal
- It is important to record at a good level in order to maximise the **signal-to-noise ratio**, but not sufficiently loud that the signal's peaks are clipped
- Normally, the first gain stage to adjust is that of the instrument itself, the next is the gain on the preamp or interface, and so on
- The gain at each stage of recording needs to be well above the noise floor but with enough headroom to be comfortably below the point of **distortion/ clipping**.

Signal-to-noise ratio

- The signal-to-noise ratio of a recording is how we describe the difference in volume between the signal you want to **capture** and the **noise**
- A poor signal-to-noise ratio will mean that noise is more prevalent in a recording
- Because the signal is quieter and is thus closer to the volume of the noise, the engineer will have to boost the volume of the signal, which also boosts the volume of the noise.

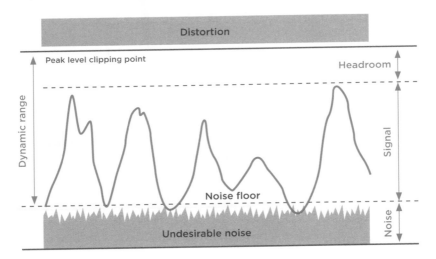

Headroom

- Headroom is the gap between the loudest peaks of your mix or audio and the point at which digital **clipping** begins
- Sometimes, analogue soft clipping is used to add warmth to a recording, but digital clipping sounds harsh and unmusical.

Direct injection

- A **DI** box converts a signal at instrument or **line level** to microphone level, and unbalanced signals to balanced signals
- DI boxes are used to eliminate the need to mic up electronic instruments, giving a direct connection to an **audio interface** or mixer.

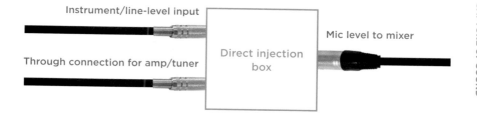

Instrument/line-level input

Mic level to mixer

Through connection for amp/tuner

Direct injection box

Plosive sounds

- **Plosive** sounds have a strong initial transient ('p','d') which can create a large disturbance in air pressure on the **diaphragm**, resulting in a 'pop' sound
- A pop filter is used to disperse the air more evenly to avoid such a quick and large diaphragm movement
- It is possible to reduce the impact of plosive sounds using **EQ** and **compression**, but by far the best solution is to re-record, or comp in the word or phrase from another part of the song.

Example microphone placements

Instrument	Microphone	Placement
Acoustic guitar	(Small diaphragm) **Condenser microphone** (to **capture** full **frequency** range/wide dynamic range/brightness) **Cardioid**.	■ Approx. 6-24 inches/ 15-60 cm ■ In front of the 12th fret of the guitar (where the neck meets the body).
Electric/ bass guitar	**Dynamic microphone** (for high SPL) Cardioid OR DI box You could also use both a microphone and a DI box and decide on the best signal later/use both.	■ Close to speaker grille ■ Placement on speaker gives brightness – centre of cone is bright, edge of cone is duller ■ If the microphone is on-axis, the sound will be brighter than when it is off-axis.

| Vocals | (Large diaphragm) **Condenser microphone** (to capture full frequency range/wide dynamic range). | ■ Performer could be up to 30cm from **pop shield**, which itself should be 8-12cm from the microphone itself

■ Use **shock mount** to isolate the microphone from vibrations through stand

■ Use pop shield to avoid capture of plosive sounds. |

Find out more about specific microphone placements for other instruments in the *AS and A Level Music Technology Study Guide* by Tim Hallas.

Synthesisers

A synthesiser is an electronic sound generator capable of creating and manipulating synthetic sounds. It has become common to use synthesisers as DAW plug-ins, but the sounds, warmth and authenticity of vintage analogue equipment are highly regarded by many.

How does a synthesiser work?

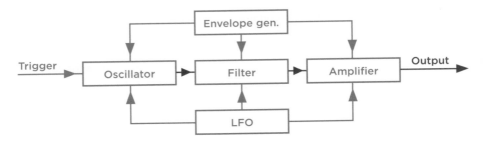

Oscillator

- The **oscillator** generates an initial sound at a pitch, and allows you to choose a wave shape
- Each has different harmonic content and thus can be used to create different **timbres**

Sawtooth

Square

Sine

- There are two tuning controls on an oscillator:
  - **Coarse-tuning** sets the pitch in semitones
  - **Fine-tuning** is measured in cents (there are 100 cents to a semitone)
- A **noise** generator creates white noise; a random signal consisting of all frequencies at an equal **amplitude**
- It is used to simulate wind or percussive sounds like cymbals, and can also be filtered to create a **sweeping** effect
- Many synthesisers have more than one **oscillator**

White noise

- **Fine-tuning** can be used to slightly detune multiple oscillators, creating a 'chorus-like' effect
- A synthesiser's polyphony tells us how many notes it can play simultaneously; a **monophonic** synthesiser can only play one note at once
- **Glide** or **portamento** controls how much a synth slides between two notes
- You can change a synthesiser's **pitch bend** range; this controls how many semitones the pitch bend wheel or **MIDI** controller will bend a note up or down by.

Filter

- The filter removes frequencies from the initial signal to shape the sound
- Synths often incorporate a **low pass filter**, as shown in the graph on page 37, which removes all of the frequencies above the cutoff frequency
- The cutoff frequency is the point at which the filter begins to remove frequencies
- Some synthesisers also include **high pass filters** or **band pass filters**.

For more on different types of filters, their parameters and graphs, turn to page 36.

Amplifier

- The **amplifier** controls the sound's volume
- Control signals such as envelopes and **LFOs** can be used to alter the volume over time.

Envelope generator

- The **envelope generator** can be used to control the **oscillator**, filter and/or **amplifier**, depending on the specific synthesiser.

The four envelope stages are:

Attack	The time taken for the parameter to increase from 0 to the maximum level.
Decay	The time taken for the parameter to decrease to the sustain level.
Sustain	The level at which the parameter is held whilst the key remains pressed.
Release	The time taken for the parameter to decrease to 0, once the key is released.

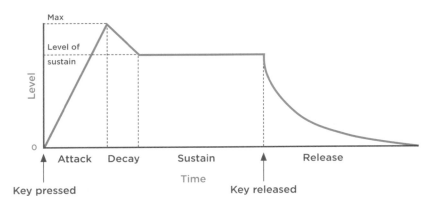

- Examples of parameters that could be controlled by an envelope include pitch, filter cutoff frequency and volume

- The envelope also plays a part in creating a sound's **timbre**; along with a signal's harmonic content, it is part of what helps us to tell a piano apart from a violin.

LFO

- Like an envelope, an **LFO (low frequency oscillator)** is a control signal used to alter a parameter over time

- Most synthesisers can use LFOs to control different modules; if controlling the oscillator, it can change the base pitch generated, creating **vibrato**

- If it is modulating the filter cutoff frequency, it will periodically change this according to the LFO wave shape.

Rate	Speed at which the **modulation** takes place; can either be synced to a note value in a **DAW** (e.g. 1/8 or a quaver) or given an absolute value in hertz, normally between around 0.05Hz and 15Hz.

- The diagram below shows a sine wave being used to modulate pitch, creating vibrato:

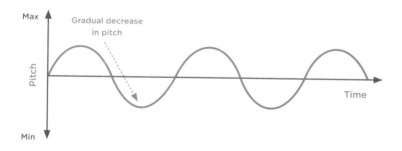

- One of the most useful features of LFOs on a DAW is the ability to sync the LFO to the main tempo of the project, creating effects that are in time with your track.

SYNTHESISERS

Types of synthesiser

- **Analogue** synthesisers use an electrical voltage to generate a signal. We can refer to the different modules on an analogue synth as being voltage-controlled; the VCO (voltage-controlled oscillator), VCF (filter) and VCA (**amplifier**)

- Digital **synthesis** uses **DSP** and computer technology to generate and manipulate a signal. Digital synthesisers can also emulate and model other equipment

- **Subtractive** synthesisers start with a harmonically rich **waveform** and use filters to remove frequencies

- Additive synthesisers layer up simple **waveforms** (e.g. sine waves) to produce a more complex wave. Hammond organs are examples of additive synthesisers.

Historically important synthesisers:

- **Moog Modular** (1965) Wendy Carlos – *Switched-On Bach*

- **Minimoog** (1969) Tubeway Army – 'Are 'Friends' Electric?' (lead line)

- **Sequential Circuits Prophet-5** (1977) Paul McCartney – 'Wonderful Christmastime', A-ha – 'Take On Me' (opening riffs), Jean-Michel Jarre – 'Fifth Rendez-vous'

- **Roland Jupiter-8 (JP-8)** (1981) Queen – 'Radio Ga Ga' (arpeggiated bassline after drum solo), Queen – 'I Want To Break Free' (synth solo from 2:06 – 2:34)

- **Roland TB-303** (1982) Phuture – 'Acid Trax' (fades in from approximately 1:05), Fatboy Slim – 'Everybody Needs A 303' (from 1:04, very audible from 2:33)

- **Yamaha DX-7** (1983) Vangelis – 'The Motion Of Stars' ('bell-like' opening synths), Brian Eno – 'Apollo: Atmospheres and Soundtracks' (most of Eno's work uses the DX7 extensively)

- **Korg M1** (1988) Des'ree – 'You Gotta Be' (acoustic guitar in opening), Black Box – 'Ride On Time' (piano from 0:20), Basement Jaxx – 'Never Say Never' (Mark Knight Remix) (piano chords).

Other electronic instruments

Theremin (1920)

- Played by moving your hands near one or two aerials
- Experienced something of a revival in the 1990s as people built them for their own use
- Creates a very pure sound with **portamento** appearing between notes because of its playing technique. Often played with a very obvious **vibrato**.

Listening
The Beach Boys – 'Good Vibrations' (0:26 -)

Hammond B3 organ (1954)

- Originally invented as a low-cost alternative to the pipe organ
- Widely used in many pop music genres from the 1960s onwards
- This tonewheel, drawbar organ is often played through a rotating Leslie speaker – the rotation speed can be altered, giving a **chorus**/phasing/**tremolo** effect.

Listening
Booker T. and The M.G.'s – 'Green Onions' (lead line)

Rhodes piano (1965)

- An electric piano that produces a sound that sounds like a cross between a bell and a vibraphone (without vibrato)
- Often played through effects pedals to produce a variety of effects similar to that of an electric guitar
- A very similar (slightly harsher) sound is produced by its main competitor, the Wurlitzer.

Listening
Herbie Hancock/Miles Davis – 'Bitches Brew'
Ray Charles – 'Shake Your Tailfeather'

Hohner Clavinet (1968)

An amplified clavichord that became synonymous with the sound of funk.

Listening
Stevie Wonder – 'Superstition'

Software synthesisers

- As computers became more powerful, **plug-in** instruments became popular because of their ability to produce the sounds of their hardware equivalent without having to purchase more than one synth!

- This is especially true of the popular vintage synths that may be hard to get hold of in playable condition, and are often very expensive due to the popularity of vintage gear amongst enthusiasts

- There remains a demand for 'vintage' **analogue** synthesisers; equipment worth very little in the late 1980s and early 1990s now sometimes sells for thousands of pounds

- In recent years, the cost of manufacturing analogue synthesisers has decreased, and manufacturers have developed and released equipment that combines analogue technology and sounds with computer control.

Benefits of software synthesisers	Benefits of analogue synthesisers
- Can be automated, **MIDI** controlled and easily sequenced - **DAWs** with a global tempo allow you to easily sync **LFOs/ arpeggiators** to a note value (this is much harder to do aurally on a hardware synth) - Better **signal-to-noise ratio** - Wide variety of presets available at the touch of a button - Can create your own presets, and share on the internet - Can use multiple instances of the plug-in - Stay in tune reliably; it is common for **analogue** synthesisers to go out of tune when they heat up - Can have more envelope stages, types of **waveform**, **oscillators** and filter types.	- Enthusiasts refer to the analogue sound as 'warm' when compared to 'harsher' or 'sterile' digital sounds; this is because of the 'flaws' associated with analogue technology – things like the tuning drifting, **noise**, aurally-pleasing **distortion** and subtle and random variations in wave shape, **amplitude** and **frequency** - Possible to use **CV/gate** systems to sync analogue equipment together; converters exist to connect analogue synthesisers to **MIDI** equipment - Your music can 'stand out from the crowd' – less reliant on presets and sounds others are using – sounds more individual - Analogue synthesisers by definition have a 'hands-on' interface – with permanently routed controls, it is easy to change settings 'on-the-fly'.

Samplers

Sampling is when you take a part of a song, single note or sound and reuse it in another context. It is common to use a sampler to either record, manipulate or playback one of these pieces of audio material (or any combination of the three). The technique of using everyday noises in music began in earnest with the Musique Concrète movement of 20th century experimental music.

The tape recorder and early sampling

- The tape recorder was the main 'instrument' for early Musique Concrète composers

- They would use it to **capture** sounds and then manipulate them by cutting and splicing the tape, making loops (by splicing the ends of a length of tape together, forming a literal loop), **reversing** the playback direction, altering the speed of playback and combining/layering sounds

- There were limitations to what could be achieved with tape, for example, it was impossible to change the speed of playback without altering the pitch

- This process formed the basis for modern-day **sampling**, and the 1960s saw the first instruments used in pop music that could play back samples.

Listening
The Beatles – 'Tomorrow Never Knows'
This song showcases a variety of tape-based manipulations, from tape loops and changing the playback speed to reversing and using **tape saturation** as a creative tool.

Mellotron (1962)

It was the Mellotron that first achieved widespread acceptance as an early sampler. It used different banks of pre-recorded tapes (one tape strip for each key) giving several choices of sound (including strings, brass, flute and choir). It was expensive, and notoriously fragile.

Listening
The Beatles – 'Strawberry Fields Forever' (opening flute)
Led Zeppelin – 'The Rain Song' (strings from 1:36)

SAMPLERS

The sampler as an instrument

- Samplers can record audio either as one-shot, single note samples or as short loops/musical excerpts
- They can then store this audio ready for playback or apply processing and sample manipulations
- Early digital samplers had limited memory in which to store samples and thus the **bit depth** and **sample rate** were lowered to save space, making the samples sound lo-fi.

For more information on digital **sampling**, bit depth and **sample rate**, turn to pages 59-61.

- Drum machines embraced early sampling technology; the samples required were short, at a single pitch, and thus did not take up much memory
- The Roland TR-909 used sampled cymbal sounds; this greatly improved the realism of the sounds compared to those synthesised on the TR-808
- Samplers often feature controls that are similar to a synthesiser, such as **LFOs** and envelopes.

Historically important samplers:

- **Fairlight CMI** (1979) Kate Bush – 'Cloudbusting' (vocal sample in bridge, steam engine sounds at end), Jean-Michel Jarre – *Zoolook* (made completely on a Fairlight CMI)
- **E-MU Emulator** (1981) Depeche Mode – 'Construction Time Again' (uses the Emulator throughout), Cutting Crew – '(I Just) Died In Your Arms Tonight' (used an Emulator stock patch for the Shakuhachi opening phrase, although was played on an Emulator II)
- **AKAI S900** (1986) Prodigy – 'Out Of Space' (drum samples) , Fatboy Slim used the S950 in 'Right Here, Right Now' and throughout *You've Come A Long Way Baby*
- **E-MU ESI Series** (1994) Famously used by Daft Punk, particularly on 'Homework'
- **Nemesys Gigasampler** (1997) This was a software sampler that held only the attack of the sample in memory and streamed the rest from a hard disk. This was revolutionary and meant that limited RAM was less of an issue, improving the quality of stored and replayed samples.

Making samples realistic

- Just like the synthesiser, it is now common to see samplers as software instruments on **DAW** software
- Two key techniques are used to make samples sound realistic:

Keyboard tracking	Spreading a single sample out across the keyboard. The sample is pitch-shifted in response to the key played; however, it is noticeable when a sound is pitch-shifted beyond a few tones.
Multisampling	Taking a sample every few notes and mapping across the keyboard so that samples are pitch-shifted across a smaller range of notes.

- When done well, it can be impossible to tell that a sound source has been sampled, just as it might be impossible to spot a well-executed edit in a multitrack recording
- When done badly, **sampling** can introduce **artefacts** such as clicks when a loop point is badly chosen.

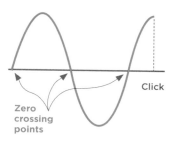

Zero crossing editing

- It is important to cut samples at a zero crossing point to avoid creating a click; you could also fade the sample out (if the edit is at the end), or use **crossfade looping**.

Manipulating and altering samples

Loop	Repeats the sample.
Transpose	Changes the starting pitch/key of a sample.
Normalise	Increases the volume to the maximum without distorting.
Stuttering	Repeating small parts of the sample to create a 'stutter' effect.
Gapping	Adding spaces between small parts of the sample.

Reverse	Playing the sample backwards.
Time stretch	Slowing down or speeding up the sample. On tape, slowing the sample down will also decrease the pitch and vice versa.
Pitch shift	Moving the entire sample up or down in pitch. On tape, a higher pitch will result in a faster sample playback and vice versa.

When working with tape, time and pitch are linked. On most samplers, when pitch-shifting a sample (such as when mapping to a keyboard), the length of the sample also changes as a side-effect. However, time stretch and pitch shift can be independently achieved with digital technology.

Destructive and non-destructive editing

- Destructive editing changes the audio file associated with the sample; processing is not normally reversible. Normally, editing in a **DAW** sample editor is destructive. Physically making changes to a tape is another example of destructive editing

- Non-destructive editing does not change the audio file, and effects or processing are normally easily removed. Channel strip plug-ins used as inserts and send effects are non-destructive.

Software samplers

- Musicians still struggle with the reliability of software-based equipment when touring, so despite the capabilities of software, hardware still has its place in the working musician's gig bag

- The line between synths and samplers has become gradually more blurred, as many synths provide sample playback or integrate fully-fledged samplers and can use sampled **waveforms** as the basis of their **synthesis** engines

- You can use synthesis functions such as filters, envelopes and **LFOs** to manipulate samples, in effect replacing the **oscillator** with a sample as a sound source

- It is also possible to apply **sampling** techniques in the arrange window on a DAW, and this can sometimes provide more flexibility in editing and manipulating a short extract of audio.

Listening
Fatboy Slim – 'Praise You' (1999)

This track is famous for the dodgy **looping** of the vowel 'oo' in the word 'should', where the loop points have been poorly chosen to create an audible step, instead of a smooth, **sustained** note. What is less well-known is that the opening backing is a series of looped samples as well, demonstrating Fatboy Slim's true abilities in sample manipulation. Fatboy Slim introduced the **sampling artefact** to make an interesting, ear-catching musical feature, and to deliberately add rhythmic interest.

The electric guitar

Just as synths are the cornerstone of electronic music, guitars (particularly electric guitars) are the driving force behind many musical styles including blues, rock and metal.

Construction

- Electric guitars started life as amplified acoustic guitars – they had a hollow body. This led to problems with feedback when amplification was turned up
- The solid-bodied guitar was introduced to combat this problem.

Pickups

- Like a microphone, a **pickup** is a **transducer**; the first part of the process of amplifying the vibration of a string is to convert the vibration into an electrical signal
- The two main types of pickup are single-coil and humbucker
- Single-coil pickups are susceptible to interference and hum, but produce a brighter, more cutting sound
- Humbucker pickups reduce interference and hum. They use two coils of opposite magnetic and electric polarity; electromagnetic **noise** hitting both coils cancels itself out.

Humbucker pickups work in a similar way to **balanced XLR** cables. To find out more about the process by which they cancel out noise, turn to page 57.

The tremolo arm

- **Tremolo** arms allow the player to adjust the pitch of the strings, making it possible to add **vibrato**, 'divebomb' effects and 'screaming' harmonics
- Because the tremolo arm affects the overall tuning of the whole guitar, locking nut and Floyd Rose tremolo systems were introduced to reduce the associated tuning problems
- Although the name suggests tremolo, the effect produced on the guitar is really a **modulation** in pitch so perhaps 'vibrato arm' would be more appropriate.

 Listening

Joe Satriani – 'Surfing With The Alien' (screaming harmonics at 1:40)

Van Halen – 'Eruption' (divebombs at 0:12 and 0:39)

Harmonics

- Harmonics occur naturally when a note is played as an oscillation on a string or tube; whilst you hear one main note, it is accompanied by other, quieter frequencies. Rather than hearing these as notes, they form part of the sound's **timbre**
- It is possible to isolate higher harmonics on stringed and wind instruments; this changes the timbre of the note, sounding 'thinner' or 'cleaner'. Harmonics have a clear, 'bell-like' tone.

 Listening

Genesis – 'Horizons' (introduction)

Yes – 'Roundabout' (opening – after the reversed piano chord)

Sequencers and digital audio workstations

Step sequencing

- In step **sequencing**, the notes are entered into a sequencer's memory one at a time onto a grid or series of buttons
- Step sequencers were built into a number of popular **analogue** synths during the 1970s; regular musical loops became a feature of the synth pop style

- They are still very popular in electronic dance styles, especially the trance music of the 1990s with its rapid arpeggios and minor scale patterns.

Listening
Robert Miles – 'Children'

Analogue sequencers

- Early sequencers sent **CV/gate** signals to trigger notes on a synthesiser
- In order to do this, a voltage was sent from the sequencer to control the opening and closing of **gates** to play notes on a synthesiser module
- Ultravox are a famous example of a band who modified their equipment in the late 1970s and early 1980s, controlling **analogue** synthesisers from their drum machines.

Listening
Ultravox – 'Vienna'

Digital sequencing

- The late 1970s brought with them a number of digitally controlled analogue sequencers, which also used voltage control but with computer memory
- During the late 1970s and early 1980s, step sequencers were included as part of the samplers produced by Synclavier and Fairlight.

MIDI

- **MIDI** was introduced in 1983, and became the standard language used by electronic musical instruments to communicate with each other

- It also provided a link to a computer; the Atari ST (1985) was built with MIDI ports

5-pin DIN MIDI port

- It was successful with amateur musicians and professional studios because it was easier to programme a sequence on the computer and send it through the MIDI ports to control a synthesiser, sampler or drum machine.

Drum machines

- Drum machines use **sequencing** technology to create rhythmic patterns
- Early drum machines relied on preset patterns
- In the late 1970s, the first programmable drum machines were introduced.

Historically important drum machines:

- **Rhythmicon** (first electronic drum machine) (1931)
- **Roland CR-78** (1978) Blondie – 'Heart Of Glass'
- **Linn LM-1** (1979) Prince – 'When Doves Cry'
- **Roland TR-808** (1980) Marvin Gaye – 'Sexual Healing'
- **Roland TR-909** (1984) Daft Punk – 'Revolution 909', Rhythm Is Rhythm – 'Strings of Life'
- **Akai MPC60** (1988) Kris Kross – 'Jump'.

Controlling MIDI and audio in modern DAWs

Quantisation and quantise values

- When working with **MIDI** data, there is likely to be an element of rhythmic imprecision that comes with the performance of a part
- Quantisation moves the timing of the beginning of a note to the nearest grid division; a note length, beat or even bar
- The numbers you see on **quantise** settings relate to the smallest divisions on the grid for quantise to 'snap' to
- The bottom number of a quantise resolution tells us how many of that note you can fit in a bar of $\frac{4}{4}$

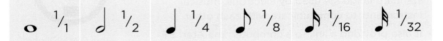

- A resolution of 1/12 refers to quaver/eighth note triplets, and 1/24 to semiquaver/sixteenth note triplets.

Percentage and swing quantise

- Percentage quantise can be used to retain some of the music's natural flexibility in timing by moving the note a percentage towards the quantise position on the grid
- Swing quantise can be used to add a **swung** feel to straight quavers or semiquavers, by slightly lengthening the first note of a pair and shortening the second. This is often denoted by a number (the note value), and a letter (the amount of swing)

- 8A means that quavers would be played with a light swing, 16E means heavily swung semiquavers.

Editing pitch and rhythm of audio

- Pitch correction plug-ins can be used to retune a vocal part. Many plug-ins allow you to set a scale to specify exactly which notes should be played
- The response time controls how quickly the plug-in tunes the notes; a response time that is too fast will create an 'R&B-style' effect

Listening

Cher – 'Believe' (1998)

This was the earliest recorded use of Auto-Tune as a creative effect, audible around 0:35 on the lyrics 'can't break through'.

Kanye West – 'Heartless' (2008)

More extreme pitch correction software is used in the song's title hook, audible at the start on the lead vocal.

- Modern **DAWs** incorporate 'flex-pitch' to change specific notes in a piano roll editor
- It is also possible to pitch shift single notes by using a plug-in that can change the note's pitch by a certain number of semitones or cents
- Audio **quantise** can be used to correct rhythms
- The transients in an audio file are analysed and they are individually time stretched to snap to a grid, as for **MIDI**
- You can also manually use the scissor tool to move audio files and single notes back into time.

Automation, balance and blend

- Balancing a mix involves finding appropriate levels and positions for the different instruments
- **Automation** can be used to control any plug-in parameter during mixing. This is useful as it is unlikely that all the parts will stay at the same volume throughout
- **Reverb** can also help to blend the whole track together, putting all of the instruments into the same acoustic space
- If a project integrates live audio recording and use of MIDI **timbres**, the live parts will have a wider dynamic range and will require **compression** to create an effective mix.

Stereo field and panning

- **Panning** is more a mixing technique than an effect, referring to the placement of sounds in the **stereo field**
- Auto-panning could be thought of as an effect – instead of placing a sound at one pan position for the whole song, auto-panning shifts the sound in the stereo field
- Stereo reverb can be used to give **mono** tracks some sense of stereo
- Panning in the 1960s was commonly polarised. Sometimes, the drum kit was on one side of the stereo image and the vocal on the other; older tracks are sometimes remastered to cater to modern stylistic conventions
- Lead vocals, bass guitars, kick drums and snare drums are normally positioned in the centre of the stereo field, and drum overheads are normally panned left and right
- If you have two guitars, or layers of backing vocals, it is common to use the stereo field to separate the parts in the mix, and keep left and right vaguely equal
- There may be questions on how the instruments in a particular recording have been panned, so ensure that you have your headphones on the right way round!
- You might have to identify pan positions, comment on how the stereo field is used in a recording, apply panning automation, or identify and/or apply doubletracking.

Dynamic processing

Dynamic processing is often rather difficult to hear in isolation – our ears can be more forgiving of changes in dynamics than changes in frequency – so examples of the following dynamic range processors will need to be rather extreme. By far the best way to become familiar with the sound of dynamic range processors is to experiment with them using your audio software or hardware units, adjusting the different parameters to see how they interact and change the sound of the music.

Compression

- A compressor reduces the dynamic range of music
- The most basic way of compressing the sound is to 'ride the fader' – when the volume gets too high, reduce the level of the fader and when it gets too low, increase the fader level

- This 'manual **compression**' was one of the ways engineers would originally have controlled the dynamic range of music
- However, it is not ideal as it takes time for the hand to respond to what the ear hears, so some peaks and troughs in volume will slip through
- A compressor automates this process by setting a level (the **threshold**) above which the compressor acts, reducing the volume of the signal by a certain amount (the **ratio**)
- After the peaks in the dynamic range have been reduced, the make-up gain boosts the whole signal
- Overall, this process 'squashes' or evens out the dynamic range of the music
- Extreme compression is audible, but when subtle, it is only really identifiable when comparing the two signals
- There is still a lot of 'riding the fader' used by engineers, but usually in the form of **automation**
- The engineer can graphically draw in changes that will then control the level of the track.

To find out more about automation and editing using a **DAW**, turn to page 31.

Compressor controls/parameters

Threshold	The volume above which a compressor begins to compress.
Ratio	**Ratio** of input volume:output volume; how much the compressor will reduce the signal by once the signal is above the **threshold**; the amount of **compression**.
Make-up gain	Compensates for the reduction in volume that occurs as part of the compression process; increases the overall volume after compression.

- Overcompression can create 'ducking' and 'pumping' effects, or accentuate unwanted quieter sounds, like breath **noises** or hiss. It also reduces the signal-to-noise ratio.

DYNAMIC PROCESSING

Listening

Kylie Minogue – 'Wow'

In the opening of this track, overcompression is used as a creative effect on the piano.

Daft Punk – 'One More Time'

When the kick drum enters, the compressor is used to create a 'pumping' or 'ducking' effect on the **sustained** brass chords from 0:48.

De-essing

- Sibilant sounds such as 'sss', 'sshh', 't', and 'oh' can be distracting in a recording
- These sounds generally exist at frequencies between 5kHz-10kHz
- De-essers can control these specific frequencies within the mix and thus reduce this sibilance.

Listening

George Michael – 'Cowboys And Angels'

This track has a lot of high-**frequency** content, deliberately emphasising the sibilance. It could probably do with a little de-essing in places (e.g. at 1:14 on 'wish').

Limiting

- **Limiters** are compressors with extreme settings
- They are used to prevent signals from increasing beyond a certain level to avoid damaging equipment or increasing beyond an acceptable limit (e.g. 0**dB**), controlling the peaks a compressor might have missed
- Limiters will have a **ratio** set as close to ∞:1 as possible (in practice this tends to be approximately 20:1). The term 'brick wall limiting' is used to describe this.

Expansion and gating

- **Expanders** work in the opposite way to a compressor – they reduce the level of signals that fall below a set **threshold**, expanding the dynamic range instead of reducing it
- They are most commonly used as **noise** reducers, by setting the threshold for the quiet sections of the music so that the background noise is reduced in level, but when the vocalist begins singing, the level rises above the threshold and is unaffected.

Noise gates

- **Noise gates** are extreme **expanders** (in the same way that **limiters** are extreme compressors) – they have a **ratio** set as close to 1:∞ as possible, reducing any signal to silence when it passes below the **threshold**
- Noise gates can be used to remove background noise as long as nothing else is playing at the same time.

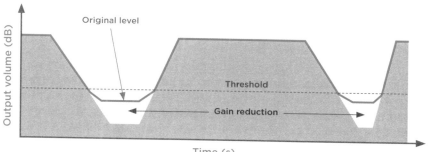

Threshold	The volume below which a noise gate silences audio. When the signal goes above the threshold, the gate opens. An expander will reduce the volume of audio that is below the threshold.

Dynamic processing and mastering

- The use of **compression** and **limiting** on a whole mix increases the perceived loudness of a track
- This has led to the so-called 'loudness wars', where there has been a trend over the past 20 years, particularly in remastered music, to create very loud masters with a very narrow dynamic range
- This can be tiring for the ear and means that musical interest needs to be generated using other production methods, such as frequently varying the instrumentation, creative use of effects, filtering and so on
- When using **analogue** technology like tape and vinyl, having a loud track helps to mask the **noise** inherent in those formats
- Loud masters are also popular when releasing music for playback on equipment with small speakers, e.g. in mobile phones and tablets
- Some streaming services now use a process called loudness normalisation. This analyses the average volume of a song and applies an offset to avoid

constantly changing the volume to compensate for louder or quieter masters. Whilst you can make your mix stand out on a CD through heavy **compression** and **limiting**, the opposite is true in this case; longer, quieter sections often lead to a larger volume offset, and thus potentially a mix that stands out more

- Engineers will often use a reference track to ensure consistency between album tracks for EQ and dynamic range.

Equalisation

Equalisation (or EQ) was originally invented to compensate for tonal inadequacies in audio equipment. It was used exclusively to correct deficiencies in the sound, thus 'equalising'. As studio equipment became more sophisticated there was no longer the same need to compensate for its inadequacies, so EQ was used more creatively.

- **Equalisation** is the process by which different **frequency** ranges are increased or decreased in volume
- An EQ will give the user a combination of various filters that can be used in conjunction with each other
- Hardware EQs are limited by the components used in the manufacture and design of the unit, including the space on the front panel for the necessary controls, but have many desirable sonic qualities
- Plug-in EQs, used in audio production software, can offer almost limitless features and combinations of filter types.

Filters

- A filter lets some of the audio signal through without changing it, but will cut or boost the signal level of a specific frequency range
- Examples of filters are low pass (LPF), high pass (HPF), band pass (BPF), and shelving filters. Semi-parametric EQ can be used to boost or cut around a frequency
- Strictly speaking, a filter just takes something away from the signal
- In practical terms, most of the filters we would use for musical applications allow us to boost as well
- It is common to see individual filters as **DAW** plug-ins; like other effects, **automation** can be used to control their individual parameters.

Filter parameters

Cutoff frequency	The cutoff frequency determines which frequencies will be passed unaffected and which frequencies will be removed.
Centre frequency	The centre frequency determines the frequency around which a **band pass filter** allows frequencies to pass through.
Gain	The gain control will determine how much cut or boost is applied to the affected frequencies.

Low pass filters

- **Low pass filters** reduce the level of all frequencies above the cutoff frequency, but let the frequencies below this value pass by unaltered
- LPFs can be heard in many dance tracks where the drum part begins sounding muffled, and gradually becomes clearer and clearer
- In this case, the cutoff frequency is gradually increasing
- LPFs can also be used to reduce hiss on a recording.

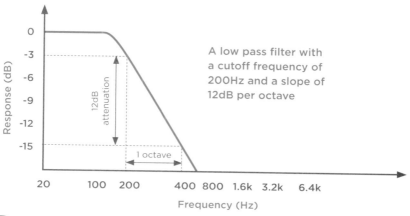

A low pass filter with a cutoff frequency of 200Hz and a slope of 12dB per octave

Listening
Madonna – 'The Power of Good-Bye'
The arpeggiated synth sound in the opening has an LPF applied, initially with a relatively low cutoff frequency. It is gradually opened up just before the vocals come in.

Fatboy Slim – 'Right Here, Right Now'

In this song, the entire mix is low pass filtered in the opening. The cutoff frequency gradually increases and more high frequencies are let through the filter. This is most audible up to 0:30, but filtering is used afterwards and throughout to add further contrast and musical interest.

High pass filters

- A **high pass filter** lets the frequencies above the cutoff frequency pass unaffected but cuts those below
- A common use of an HPF is as a rumble filter, where it is set between 80 and 150Hz to eliminate unwanted low **frequency** sounds – many mixers include a switch on each channel for this.

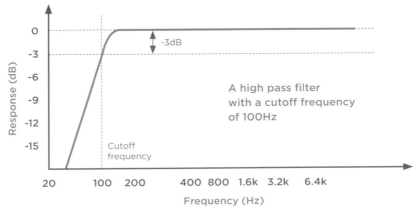

A high pass filter with a cutoff frequency of 100Hz

Listening

Stardust – 'Music Sounds Better With You'

The opening of the track sounds very thin because an HPF is cutting all the low end. The filter is turned off at 0:16, at which point the full frequency range can be heard.

Band pass filters

- A **band pass filter** is essentially a combination of an LPF and an HPF, where any frequencies outside the scope of the LPF and HPF pass unaffected
- They are used in **wah wah** pedals, where the centre frequency is swept to give the characteristic effect (see page 51).

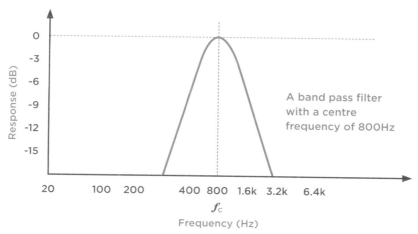

A band pass filter with a centre frequency of 800Hz

Semi-parametric EQ

- You can use a semi-parametric EQ to boost or cut around a variable centre frequency
- It is useful for adjusting the amplitude of a specific frequency or frequency range, but without altering all the frequencies above and below.

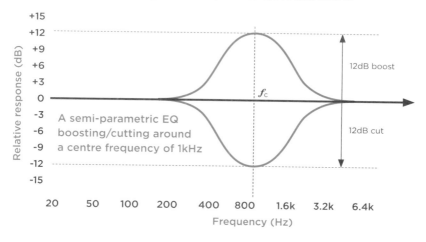

A semi-parametric EQ boosting/cutting around a centre frequency of 1kHz

Shelving filters

- Shelving filters allow the user to cut or boost the signal beyond a specific **frequency**, which is then evenly applied until the end of the audio spectrum, leaving the rest of the signal unaffected; their graphs look a bit like shelves

- These are the tone controls most commonly used on consumer audio equipment and the treble/bass controls on guitar **amplifiers**.

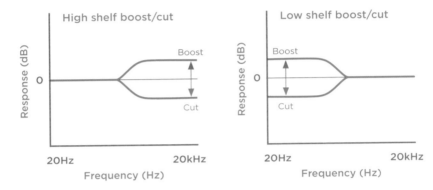

Effects

There are a variety of different effects that are commonly used in music technology. Their purposes differ; some are primarily used to create a coherent mix, and others more creatively. Many of these effects share three core parameters:

Wet	The amount of the signal from the effect.
Dry	The amount of the signal without the effect.
Bypass	Switches the unit or plug-in on/off so you can compare the signal to its unaffected version, or automate it during a track.

Reverb

Reverberation (reverb) is a naturally occurring phenomenon that gives our brains lots of information about the space we are in, even if we cannot see the space. Reverb happens when a sound reflects off its surrounding surfaces, then these reflections again reflect off the surfaces, then the process continues creating a 'wash' of overlapping echoes. **These echoes briefly remain audible even after the initial sound source has been taken away.**

■ Unless the space is very large, we don't hear these reflections as distinct echoes

■ We simply perceive a sense of space – our brains subconsciously decode the information to tell us that we are in, for example, a large, concrete room with few furnishings, or a small lounge with sofas and heavy curtains

■ Reverb has been included on recordings, by accident or design, since sound **capture** was invented; unless a sound is captured in an anechoic chamber, it is impossible to avoid capturing some of the sound of the recording space

■ Close miking helps to eliminate most, but not all of the sound of the room.

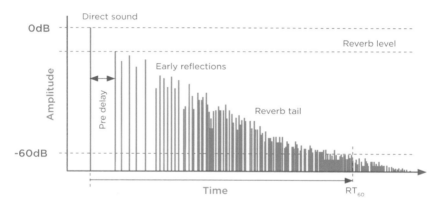

Reverb time	The amount of time taken for the **reverb** to fully **decay** to the point that we can no longer hear it. This is sometimes called RT_{60}, and is measured at the point the reverb is 60dB quieter than the original signal.

Live rooms

■ A room that is chosen to act as a recording room because of its acoustic properties is called a 'live room'

■ Engineers would place the musician(s) in a booth, room, chamber or hall that had an appropriate reverb character; this sounds very natural, but cannot be removed after the initial sound capture

■ Having a selection of live rooms is not within the budget of most studios and cannot be reproduced when the performers play at different venues, so it was not long before engineers sought new methods of producing artificial reverb.

Plate reverb

- Plate **reverb** is achieved by feeding an audio signal through a thin metal plate suspended in a frame
- The reverb time can be adjusted by damping the vibrations using felt pads
- Plate reverb was used in many recordings throughout the 1960s and 1970s; it gives a distinctive, rich-sounding reverb due to the sound being fed through a metallic plate
- It was most commonly used on vocals and drum sounds, and is still preferred to the digital alternatives by some engineers today
- The EMT 140 was a famous plate reverb, manufactured in the late 1950s.

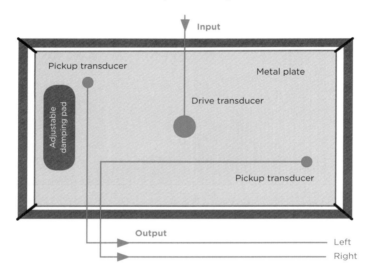

Spring reverb

- A cheaper, more practical, but less sonically desirable alternative to plate reverb is spring reverb; these units operate on the same physical principles as plate reverbs, but replace the plate with a loose spring
- They are still frequently used in guitar amps, as you will hear if you knock a spring reverb-equipped amp a little too hard!
- Spring reverb has a more metallic and less rich sound than plate reverbs
- The Fender Twin Deluxe Reverb guitar **amplifier** (released in 1963) was one of the first with a built-in spring reverb.

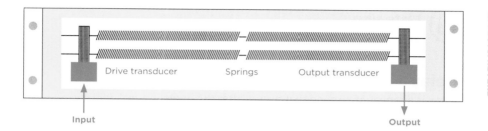

Drive transducer   Springs   Output transducer

Input   Output

Gated reverb

- Using a lot of reverb on percussion sounds can muddy a mix; if a reverb is fed through a noise gate, the tail is abruptly cut off, which prevents this from becoming an issue
- This is a rather dramatic effect that became closely associated with the classic rock sound of the 1980s.

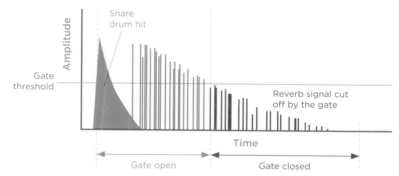

Listening
Phil Collins – 'In The Air Tonight'

The classic example of gated reverb on a big drum sound – listen to the drum fill at 3:40. The abrupt cutting of the reverb tail can be heard on the snare throughout the rest of the track.

Reverse reverb

- Created by playing the reverb tail backwards
- Modern day reverb plug-ins can create reverse reverb at the push of a button
- In the 1960s, this would have been created by recording the reverb to tape and then playing it backwards.

EFFECTS: DELAY

Listening
The Only Ones – 'Miles From Nowhere'
(percussion sounds from 1:57)

Delay

Delay is a repeat of a sound that occurs after the original signal. Initially, **analogue** delays would record the sound onto tape or use a bucket brigade chip to create a time delay. Nowadays, delay units **capture** sound digitally and replay, storing the original sound in memory and making the delay straightforward to manipulate.

Analogue delay

Tape delay

- The Echoplex was one of the first portable delay units; it recorded the original sound onto magnetic tape and then played it back
- The delay time could be changed by moving the position of the playback head
- The delay lost some of the high-**frequency** content of the original, giving it a 'warm' sound. Many modern digital delay effects try to emulate this analogue warmth
- The tape would gradually degrade, and eventually need replacing.

Listening
Queen – 'Brighton Rock'
The solo uses an Echoplex to create delays, which Brian May uses to create counterpoint and harmonies.

For more about the properties of analogue tape, turn to page 67.

Bucket brigade delay

- Later **analogue delays** used bucket brigade chips to store the original sound
- Each stage 'hands' the signal off to the next stage, much as in an old-school firefighter 'bucket brigade' in which water was passed along a line from bucket to bucket in order to reach the fire!
- The signal is held in each capacitor (or 'bucket') briefly and then moved on to the next virtual 'holding place'. This has the effect of delaying the signal in time with the clock

- These chips were much more convenient and reliable than tape, but were noisy – the longer the delay, the more **noise**.

SLAPBACK DELAY

- Slapback delay was originally an analogue delay with a single repeat after approximately 80-200ms
- It's an almost percussive effect, and the repeat is generally at a fairly high level so as to be noticeable
- It is heard on many rock'n'roll recordings of the 1950s, and was used to thicken vocals and electric guitars.

Listening
Elvis Presley – 'Mystery Train' (electric guitar)
John Lennon – 'Instant Karma!' (vocals)

Digital delay

- Digital delay stores the original sound in memory. Because it is stored digitally, it is more straightforward to manipulate.

Delay time	The gap between each repeat. Often measured in milliseconds, but software plug-ins can sync the delay to a note value in time with the tempo.

- Digital **delays** make synchronising the delay to the main tempo of a **DAW** easy, and most plug-ins will allow you to select a note value for a delay time (e.g. a minim or 1/2). This is commonly used in dance music
- U2's guitarist The Edge uses tempo-synchronised delay a great deal in creating his guitar textures.

Listening
U2 – 'Where The Streets Have No Name'

Multi-tap delay

- Multi-tap delay allows the user to set several different delay times in one effect (e.g. repeats at 200, 300 and 450ms); essentially it is several delay units in one.

Ping pong/stereo delay

- A stereo or 'ping pong' delay unit gives you the option to pan the delayed sound, either in relation to itself or the original single
- Sometimes, a multi-tap delay unit may pan each 'tap' in a different direction, and allow you to adjust other parameters associated with the volume and filtering.

Listening
Martha and the Muffins – 'Echo Beach' (opening synth)

Doubling effects

- Delay can be heard as a discrete echo if the delay time is set somewhere around 40–50ms or more
- If it is set at about 40ms or less, it has a doubling effect – it thickens the signal, sounding like two simultaneous versions of the original
- Delay can also be used to create a wider stereo image; if one stereo channel is delayed, the part or instrument can seem wider.

BENEFITS OF DELAY PLUG-INS

Analogue delays are often emulated as software plug-ins. There are a number of benefits to using a software plug-in over an analogue hardware unit:

- Easy to automate and control with MIDI
- Possible to sync delay time to DAW global tempo
- Accurate control of delay time in milliseconds
- Possible to store, share and download presets
- No issues with maintenance (compared to tape-based analogue delays)

Modulated delay effects

These effects all rely on the periodic modulation of the delay time. An LFO is used to control how much the wet signal is delayed by, and this changes over time.

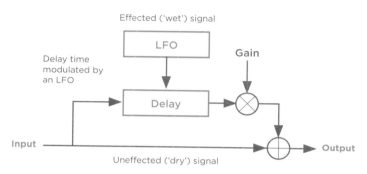

LFO rate	Speed at which the **modulation** takes place; can either be synced to a note value or given an absolute value in hertz.

Chorus

- **Chorus** originally took its name from the way it made one voice/instrument sound like a chorus of voices/instruments

- This effect delays a copy of the original signal, playing the delayed version alongside the clean signal to give the effect of more than one instrument playing at the same time

- When an LFO is used to delay a signal by a small and varying amount of time, this affects the pitch; you could say that we are adding vibrato to the wet signal

- This simulates the subtle pitch and timing differences when a number of singers or instrumentalists perform together

- For a subtle effect, the rate control is generally set quite low. The effect will just give a sense of life or movement to a signal, imbuing it with a subtle detuning effect

- If the rate value is high, it can create a 'bubbling' or 'underwater' effect

- Chorus is often used on clean electric guitar, fretless bass and synth pad tracks.

Listening

Marillion – 'Sugar Mice' (subtle to thicken/'warm up' guitar sound)

Camel – 'Nimrodel/The Procession/The White Rider' (more extreme, underwater sound)

Flanger

- **Flanger** gives a 'swirling', 'whooshing' or 'jet plane' effect, depending on the rate setting
- It generates a **sweeping**, pitched sound in time with the **LFO**
- An extreme setting gives a 'jet plane' effect, and is often used on distorted guitar
- When it is applied to just the reverb or delay of an effected signal rather than the signal itself, it can produce a subtler, 'shimmering' effect.

Listening

Queen – 'Keep Yourself Alive' (guitar riff)

Seal – 'Bring It On' (opening vocal line)

Phaser

- Phaser gives a similar audible effect to flanging, but is generally subtler
- The effect is created as the two signals combine in varying ways
- It can make a sound 'shimmer' at subtle settings – sounding a little similar to chorus, but more like a filter with an LFO applied sweeping through the frequency range, rather than like two voices/instruments playing at once
- It can be used to add movement to distorted guitar parts.

Listening

Billy Joel – 'Just The Way You Are' (Fender Rhodes)

Although phaser is included in the 'modulated delay' section, it is actually a filtering effect. This is because it is the phase of the wet signal that is altered rather than the delay time, creating interesting phase cancellation effects as the wet and dry signals combine.

Electric guitar effects

Guitar effects come in the form of stompboxes, which are individual effects units in the form of floor-mounted boxes, activated by stomping on a switch. Stompboxes were the original guitar effects units, but went out of favour a little in the late 1980s and early 1990s when multi-effects units became widely available. Stompboxes do provide more routing and editing flexibility, and have regained their popularity over the last decade.

Distortion

- **Distortion** was originally achieved by overloading the circuitry at some point in the **signal chain**. When the gain is increased, the peaks and troughs of the **waveform** are clipped, and the distorted signal has more harmonics

- Later distortion effects were incorporated into guitar amps, or as stompboxes

- Most recently, distortion effects are used as **DAW** plug-ins, sometimes emulating other hardware

- **Valve amplifiers** were used almost exclusively until the late 60s/early 70s when solid- state amplifiers began to be used

- Solid-state amplifiers used **transistors** in their construction rather than valves

- Transistors were cheaper, smaller and more reliable

- This made amplifiers more efficient, which had an impact on their affordability and size

- There has been resurgence in the use of valve amplifiers as they soft clip the signal, giving a warmer **overdrive**. Solid-state amplifiers exhibit **clipping** that gives a harsher overdrive.

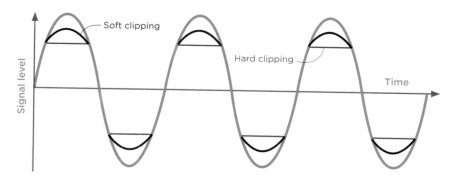

Fuzz	■ **Fuzz** was made famous by Jimi Hendrix and his use of the 'Fuzz Face' pedal
	■ It has a raw edge to it and works better with solo lines than with chords because simultaneously sounding notes all interfere with each other, merging in a dissonant fashion.

Listening
Jimi Hendrix – 'Purple Haze'

Overdrive	■ **Overdrive** is the term commonly used to describe a form of **distortion** that is smoother than fuzz and is often used for chordal passages and riffs
	■ It is often the 'crunch' setting on amps, giving 'grit' and more 'guts'
	■ It is often used for blues rhythm playing and, at higher gain settings, lead guitar work.

Listening
Chuck Berry – 'Johnny B. Goode'

Distortion	■ **Distortion**, as well as being the generic term for all three effects, can be thought of as the more extreme of the three
	■ It is used in heavy rock and metal and for lead guitar work
	■ It usually has a higher gain setting than overdrive, making it less suitable for full chords, but very suitable for heavy power-chord riffs
	■ The generic 'scooped' **EQ** (where the bass and treble are boosted while the mids are cut) guitar sound of American metal bands is one of the more famous distorted sounds, used by bands such as Metallica and DragonForce.

Listening
Metallica – 'Enter Sandman'

Parameters on distortion effects

Gain	The drive, giving the amount of distortion.
Output	The volume of the output signal (after distortion) to compensate for the increase in gain necessary to achieve distortion.
Tone	Controls the cutoff **frequency** of a **low pass filter**.

Guitar amp simulators

- Amp simulators can be used to emulate different guitar and **amplifier** sounds and the effects that go with it such as spring **reverb**, **vibrato**, and **tremolo**

- It is possible to DI a guitar and simulate the sound of it going through an amplifier and miked up speaker cabinet.

Wah wah

- **Wah wah** is commonly used in funk music and to make guitar solos sound more interesting. The effect sounds like its name; it is onomatopoeic

- It is created by **sweeping** the centre **frequency** of a **band pass filter**.

 Listening
Jimi Hendrix – 'Voodoo Child (Slight Return)'

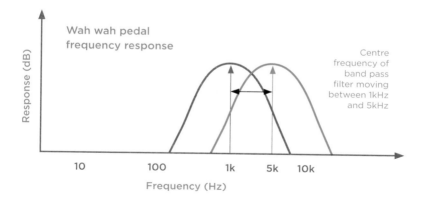

Wah wah pedal frequency response

Centre frequency of band pass filter moving between 1kHz and 5kHz

Response (dB)

Frequency (Hz)

Vibrato and tremolo

Other **modulation** effects combine wet and dry signals, but vibrato and tremolo consist only of the signal to which the effect has been applied.

- **Vibrato** modulates the pitch of the signal, using an **LFO**
- It sounds like the natural vibrato created by vocalists, or a guitarist moving their finger on the fretboard.

 ### Listening
Percy Sledge – 'When A Man Loves A Woman'
(hammond organ)

- **Tremolo** modulates the volume of the signal using an LFO
- It sounds like the note is fading in and out periodically.

 ### Listening
Nancy Sinatra – 'Bang Bang (He Shot Me Down)'
(electric guitar)

Historically, **modulation** effects would have been created using tape machines or rotary speakers.

Modulation using tape recorders

- The recording would be duplicated and played simultaneously on two tape machines
- Hand pressure was applied to the supply reel of one of the tape recorders which slowed it down slightly. This created a slight **delay**, along with a variation in pitch
- When combined, the signals from both tape recorders created a 'flange'-like modulation effect.

The Leslie cabinet/rotary speaker

- The Leslie cabinet contains a rotating horn, with two modes; **tremolo** (faster) or chorale (slower); this creates a slight shift in pitch and changes in volume and tone as the speaker spins, creating the perception of modulation
- In physics, this is called the Doppler Effect
- The Leslie cabinet was commonly used with the Hammond Organ, and is often reproduced in the form of 'Rotary' software plug-ins.

Vocal effects

Vocoders

- Vocoders analyse an incoming signal (the modulator) and apply elements of this signal to a carrier signal
- In practical use, the modulator is often the human voice and the carrier is a synth **timbre**
- The resulting sound is a 'robotic' voice that follows whatever pitch is played on the synth – it almost sounds like the synth is talking.

Listening
Pet Shop Boys – 'Shopping'

A vocoder is used in the chorus to double up with the lead vocal on "We're S.H.O.P.P.I.N.G., we're shopping".

Lo-fi effects

Telephone EQ

- A **band pass filter** or a **high pass filter** can be used to restrict the **frequency** range of a part
- This can make it sound like a telephone
- This is a common effect applied to vocal parts to provide contrast.

Listening
Muse – 'Feeling Good' (second verse)

Bit Distortion

- Lowering the **bit depth** leads to **distortion** of audio; the track can sound 'electronic' or 'lo-fi'. 'Bitcrusher' effects are often available as **DAW** plug-ins
- They recreate the alias tones that are a product of the **sample rate** and bit depth being too low
- Because of this, they can be used to emulate the sound of early **sampling** technology.

Listening
La Roux – 'Bulletproof' (synth sounds)

ACOUSTICS, MONITORING, LEADS AND SIGNALS

Other common lo-fi sounds include samples of vinyl crackle, **noise** and hiss.

Listening
Moby – 'Why Does My Heart Feel So Bad?'
Moby uses a vocal sample from a gospel song; the sample has audible noise on it, but he uses this as a creative device to avoid the track sounding 'sterile'.

Acoustics, monitoring, leads and signals

As well as understanding how recording, effects and processing work, you need to have some knowledge of acoustics, and an understanding of the theory behind studio monitors, cables and connectors, and signals.

Acoustics

- The way the surfaces in a room absorb, reflect and diffuse sound gives us our perception of that space

To find out more about how sound reflects in a room to create **reverb**, turn to pages 40-41.

- A room with lots of hard surfaces will be reflective, and a room with lots of soft surfaces (carpets, curtains, sofas and so on) will be less so
- The more reflective the room, the longer the reverb time (RT_{60})
- Acoustic treatment can help to ensure the accurate **capture** and **monitoring** of audio without unwanted **colouration** from the room.

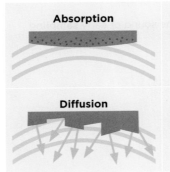

Absorption	
	- The surface doesn't reflect all of the sound waves back – it takes in some of the sound energy.
Diffusion	
	- Diffusion scatters sound waves over a wide area.

- Using acoustic treatment to control absorption, reflection and diffusion can help to solve issues such as flutter echoes, standing waves and comb filtering.

Reflection and standing waves

- Sound waves bounce off any reflective surfaces in a space
- This can make the room very reverberant if there are reflective surfaces, but it also might be too dry if there aren't any
- To make a room less reflective, soft material or acoustic treatment is added to the walls
- Reflections can cause cancellation or an increase in **amplitude** for a sound wave at a specific **frequency**
- We use acoustic treatment to prevent standing waves from affecting our recordings in a live room or our perception of frequencies in a control room.

Standing wave reflection causes phase cancellation

Wall

Loudspeaker

Standing wave reflection causes an increase in amplitude

Wall

Loudspeaker

Isolation booths

- Isolation booths are normally acoustically treated and insulated
- These booths are normally rooms within a room and have a dual purpose; isolating the performer from other instruments that could mean that **spill** is recorded onto that track, and isolating that musician from creating spill on another!
- This tends to be most important when recording drums (which often spill onto other tracks because of their volume), and vocals (which need to be the most isolated)

ACOUSTICS, MONITORING, LEADS AND SIGNALS

- You can also use screens to increase the separation between different instruments when recording them at the same time.

Monitor speakers

- Studio monitors have a relatively flat **frequency** response, meaning they don't emphasise particular frequencies.

'LOST IN TRANSLATION'

If you mix on speakers that aren't completely accurate, some frequencies will be reproduced louder or quieter than they should be. You are likely to boost or cut these frequencies further when preparing your mix, and when the mix is played back on other speakers, the problem frequencies will either be lacking or over-emphasised; we call this issue 'translation'.

- Studio monitors normally have two separate speakers within them; a tweeter and a woofer
    - The tweeter is designed to handle high frequencies (2kHz-20kHz), and the woofer everything else below this
    - Some audio systems might also use a sub-woofer, which handles very low frequencies (below 100Hz)
- Some studios use three-way monitors for even greater accuracy
- A crossover is used to separate out the signals for the speakers so that the tweeter doesn't get any of the signal meant for the sub-woofer. It basically works as a series of filters – a high pass filter for the tweeter and a low pass filter for the subwoofer.

ACOUSTICS, MONITORING, LEADS AND SIGNALS

Cables and connections

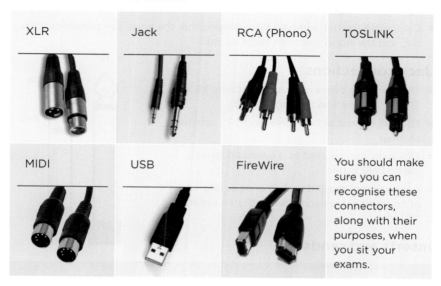

XLR	Jack	RCA (Phono)	TOSLINK

MIDI	USB	FireWire	You should make sure you can recognise these connectors, along with their purposes, when you sit your exams.

Unbalanced and balanced connections

- **XLR** cables and TRS jacks are what we call **balanced** connectors
- They cancel out **noise** picked up as part of the cable run

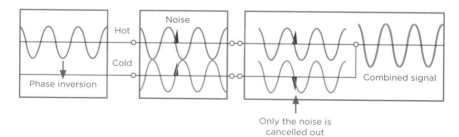

Phase inversion — Hot / Cold — Noise — Combined signal

Only the noise is cancelled out

- A balanced cable contains three connections – a hot (+), cold (-) and a ground
- The cold signal is a phase inverted version of the hot signal
- Noise is picked up equally on the hot and cold signals. This noise is in phase, but the signal is out of phase

ACOUSTICS, MONITORING, LEADS AND SIGNALS

- When both of the signals reach their destination, the cold is phase inverted again. At this time, the signal is in phase, but the noise is now out of phase
- Combining the hot and cold signal means that the noise completely cancels out, and the signal becomes twice as loud.

Jack connections

- There are two types of jack connection; TS and TRS (tip-sleeve and tip-ring-sleeve)
- TS jacks consist of two wires, and TRS consists of three
- TRS jacks can be used as a balanced, or as a stereo connection
- A variation of the TRS jack is used as one end of an insert cable connected with two separate TS jacks.

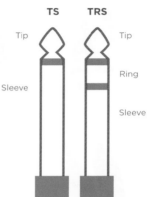

Inserts and sends

Insert effects	Send effects
Processors that replace the original signal with a new processed signal	Processors that have two signals: the dry and the wet. The dry signal is still present with an additional wet signal
<ul><li>Inserts are used to add a processor or effect as part of the channel strip in series with a track's signal</li><li>They tend to be used for processors such as **gates**, compressors and **EQs**</li><li>A processor applied to an insert will only function on the track it is inserted on.</li></ul>	<ul><li>Sends are used to route a part's signal via another channel (a bus or auxiliary track)</li><li>You can send some, none or all of the track's signal to an effects bus</li><li>Reverb and delay are the most frequently and effectively used auxiliary effects</li><li>The output of the effects bus (the 'wet' signal) is returned to the DAW's output, where it is mixed with the direct signal ('dry').</li></ul>

Signal flow for an insert effect

Signal flow for a send effect

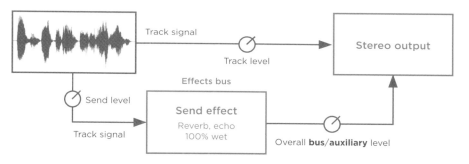

Analogue and digital recording

Digital recording has revolutionised the recording, mixing, producing and just about every other process involved in creating, distributing and listening to music.

- An **analogue waveform** is a representation of the changes in air pressure which are a result of the vibrations created when we make a sound
- Microphones convert the changes in air pressure to an electrical signal – this is an analogue signal, because its **amplitude** can have any value between the minimum and maximum
- A digital signal can only have values of 0 and 1, or on and off
- It uses these values to store a representation of the signal's amplitude as numerical data.

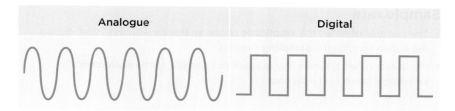

Analogue to digital conversion

- The process of **analogue** to digital conversion involves us taking digital samples of the momentary amplitude of a **waveform**

- A continuous analogue signal is converted into a series of binary numbers.

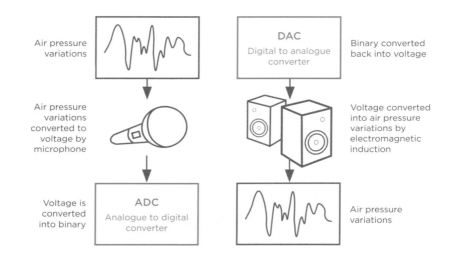

The diagram below shows a digitally sampled waveform.

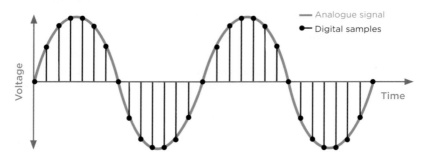

Sample rate

- The number of times the **amplitude** of the **analogue** signal is 'read' during the conversion/digital **sampling** process

- Measured in hertz, where 1Hz is equal to 1 sample of the **waveform**'s amplitude taken every second

- **Sample rates** of 44.1kHz (CD quality) and 48kHz (DVD quality) are common
- At CD quality, this means that the amplitude of the waveform is being read 44,100 times every second!
- Other higher sample rates exist, but they are less common; audio enthusiasts often argue that recordings at a higher sample rate sound better, but the limitations of human hearing means you would be very unlikely to hear any difference, even with very high-quality playback equipment
- The sample rate determines the **frequency** response of the piece of equipment – the higher the sample rate, the greater the highest frequency **captured**.

Bit depth

- The level of detail the amplitude is measured to for each sample
- It provides a snapshot of the amplitude of the waveform at the instant when the sample is taken
- The higher the **bit depth**, the more detail with which you can measure the amplitude of the analogue waveform and the greater the dynamic range and therefore the **signal-to-noise ratio**
- CD quality is 16 bit, but 24 bits are also commonly seen in digital audio. A bit depth of 24 is useful as when working on a project, the noise on multiple tracks soon adds up.

Nyquist's Theorem

- States that the sample rate of a digital system should be twice the highest frequency captured
- A sample rate of 44.1kHz (or 44,100Hz) more than adequately captures the top end of the human hearing range at 20kHz (20,000Hz).

Aliasing

- When the sample rate is not high enough, aliasing can occur
- Frequencies above the Nyquist frequency are captured and incorrectly recreated within the audible range below the Nyquist frequency
- These inaccuracies manifest as unwanted artefacts in the reproduced signal.

Discussing frequency response

- A frequency response graph shows us the frequencies that are captured by a microphone, and how much louder or quieter they are compared to the actual sound

- It shows whether frequencies are captured louder or quieter than they should be by the amount of difference in **dB** either side of 0 on the Y-axis
- The graph below shows the frequency response of a Shure SM58 microphone:

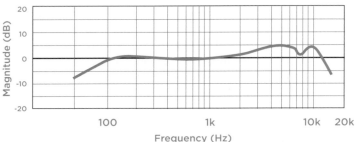

- We can see from the graph that there is a presence peak between around 4000Hz and 7000Hz. This can help the signal to cut through the mix, giving clarity and brightness. There is a reduced boost between 7000Hz and 8000Hz to control shrill-sounding high frequencies and sibilance, along with a roll off of high frequencies above 10kHz, meaning the **capture** would be less detailed. There is also a low frequency roll off below 100Hz, avoiding the capture of rumble.

Noise and interference in analogue and digital systems

- Digital signals are less susceptible to interference than **analogue** signals
- If an analogue signal picks up **noise**, this forms part of the **waveform**
- However, a digital signal is still identifiable as 0 or 1, and doesn't degrade in quality if it picks up noise.

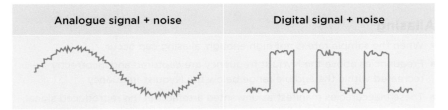

Recording media

Each format has its own characteristics and process by which audio is recorded, stored and reproduced. You need to know about, and make comparisons between different recording formats; in particular, vinyl, tape and CD. You should also have an understanding of digital audio formats such as WAV and MP3.

Studio recording formats

Analogue multitrack tape

- A cassette tape contains four tracks, arranged as 'lanes' on a tape. The four tracks represent left and right for the A and B sides of the cassette

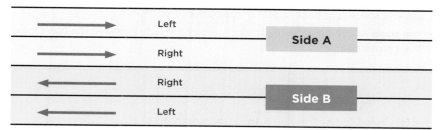

- Studio multitrack tape is wider; providing more 'lanes'; we can record independently onto each of the tracks at the same time, or at different times when **overdubbing**

- The wider the tape and the faster it runs, the higher the quality of audio reproduction

- This means less hiss and a better high **frequency** response

- Commercially, 2" tape was the widest available format, and as well as domestic 0.25" tape, widths for studio and multitrack machines included 0.5" and 1".

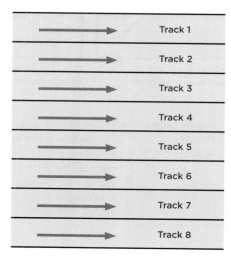

An eight-track tape

TAPE SATURATION

- An overloaded magnetic tape is said to be saturated
- Saturation occurs when the signal is too loud when entering the record head, and an increase in the input volume cannot produce an equivalent increase in magnetisation
- Slight **tape saturation** sounds similar to mild **compression** and is often a desirable quality of tape recording that is emulated by digital plug-ins.

Editing early recordings on tape

- In the 1960s, to make edits on **analogue** tape, it was necessary to physically cut and splice (put back together again) the tape
- The angle of the cut gave the smoothness of the fade between the two tapes, like a crossfade.

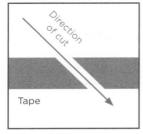

Cut both tapes/
sections at an angle

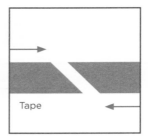

Slide the edited sections
of tape together

Join the sections
together

Digital tape (1980s, 1990s)	• DASH (digital audio stationary head) recorders were introduced in the early 1980s. They were so called because in other digital tape recorders, in order to transfer the data onto the tape, the record head rotates along with the tape movement. They could record two channels of audio on 1/4 inch tape, and 24 or 48 tracks on 1/2 inch tape

	▪ DAT (digital audio tape) was popular in studios, particularly in the 1980s and 1990s for final mixes, as a studio mastering medium. It formed the basis for professional recording in the 1990s as part of an all-digital signal chain at 12 bit/32kHz and 16 bit at 32kHz, 44.1kHz or 48kHz
	▪ Tape ADAT used VHS tapes and thus was a cost-effective multitrack solution. It was largely superseded by hard disk recording and digital audio workstations.
Hard disk recorders (1990s)	▪ In the 1990s, it was common to see hard disk recorders form part of studio setups, as it gradually replaced tape-based digital recording
	▪ Initially, costs were prohibitive, but by the mid-1990s, hard disk price decreases and increases in capacity meant that the technology was commonly seen in the majority of studios as a preferred way of working
	▪ Some hard drive recorders ultimately facilitated non-linear and non-destructive editing
	▪ The more portable devices were used for location recording
	▪ Nowadays, the DAW, smaller memory card recorders and laptops have superseded this.
DAWs	▪ Early DAWs in the mid-1990s were theoretically capable of editing more tracks or larger files but were limited by the hard disk technology of the time
	▪ Hard disks were small; large drives with faster read/write speeds to facilitate larger scale multitracking were expensive and not seen outside top-end professional studios
	▪ Since 2000, the development of the DAW has accelerated with associated improvements in computer processor speeds and increasing amounts of RAM and hard disk space. Work previously only possible in professional studios in the 1970s and 1980s can often be carried out on a laptop in a bedroom.

Consumer audio formats

Vinyl

- Vinyl records were first popular in the 1950s, but the format is still in demand today
- Many vinyl records have become collectable items, and some limited-edition records on particular labels can be worth lots of money
- Pressing a record involves engraving a copy of an acoustic waveform onto vinyl
- A stylus then moves in a groove as the disc is rotated. The vibrations are converted into an electrical signal
- Each side of the groove corresponds to a separate signal to create a stereo image
- Record labels continued to release vinyl records in both **mono** and stereo in the 1960s, as stereo did not become standard until later in the decade
- Low frequencies have to be reduced on the record to prevent the stylus from moving too much, and so **EQ** is applied when playing a record back to return the frequencies to the correct level
- Vinyl records were played at different speeds, measured in RPM (revolutions per minute) depending on their size
- 12" LPs were played at 33 1/3 RPM, and singles at 45 RPM. Early shellac records released up until the mid-1950s played at 78 RPM.

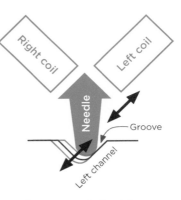

The movement of a stylus on the surface of a record

Advantages	Disadvantages
<ul><li>Enthusiasts argue that records sound more authentic/'warmer'</li><li>Some DJs still use vinyl records to beat-match and scratch</li><li>There has been a recent resurgence in the popularity of vinyl</li><li>Bands sometimes release on vinyl for kudos</li><li>Record sleeve artwork is still appreciated by many fans.</li></ul>	<ul><li>Sound quality can deteriorate towards the record's centre because of the turntable's constant rotation speed</li><li>Not very portable</li><li>Easy to scratch, which causes the needle to jump</li><li>Dust affects the sound, causing crackle; this is unfortunate as vinyl creates a static charge attracting it!</li><li>Prone to warping if exposed to heat</li><li>Prone to rumble at less than 30Hz.</li></ul>

Cassette tapes

- Cassette tapes were first popular in the 1970s
- They use the same technology as studio multitrack tape, but miniaturised and with fewer tracks
- Particles of iron oxide on the surface of the tape are magnetised by the signal from the recording head of a tape recorder. The polarisation of these particles represents the audio signal
- The playback head 'reads' the magnetic information and converts it back into an electrical signal for amplification
- The erase head of a tape recorder uses a strong permanent magnet that is placed near the tape to reset the polarisation of the iron oxide particles.

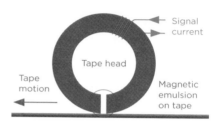

Advantages	Disadvantages
- Initially cheaper than vinyl records, but now more expensive due to lack of demand - Difficult to scratch or damage the surface of a tape as it is protected in a case - Easy to copy with 'high speed dubbing' - Longer recording times than vinyl LPs - More portable than vinyl records.	- Sometimes get tangled or snap; this can damage the tape and cause loss of parts of the audio - Recorders need to be cleaned with a head cleaner cassette as the oxide had a tendency to rub off the tape - The quality of the recording degrades with each playing, and if stored in strong magnetic fields - Susceptible to hiss, hence the **noise** reduction technologies developed by Dolby and dbx - Wow and flutter occurred with small variations in motor speed causing variations in pitch - Prone to print through; the music is heard as an echo before it actually plays.

CD audio

- CD stands for 'Compact Disc'
- It is an optical disc that stores data as pits on a disk read by a laser; recordable CDs use a laser to burn pits into a photosensitive coating
- CDs can hold 74–80 minutes of stereo LPCM audio (at 16 bit/44,100Hz)
- They can also store up to 700mb of data.

Advantages	Disadvantages
<ul><li>Better **signal-to-noise ratio** than tape or vinyl, with a wider dynamic range</li><li>Don't degrade with multiple playings</li><li>Cheaper to manufacture than tape and vinyl</li><li>Better **frequency** response</li><li>Quick and easy access to tracks because of track indexing</li><li>Easy to transfer music from CD to computer</li><li>Longer playing time and more portable than vinyl records.</li></ul>	<ul><li>Scratching can cause issues with a large amount of data and render sections of discs unplayable</li><li>Some **analogue** enthusiasts consider the sound of CD as 'brittle' and 'unmusical', preferring the warmth of vinyl.</li></ul>

Compressed digital formats

- Since the late 1990s, compressed digital audio formats have become more prevalent
- MP3 encoders compress audio data very effectively, significantly reducing the file size when compared to an uncompressed audio file
- There is a pay-off in terms of frequency content and dynamic detail, some of which is lost
- This is audible when listening to MP3s through higher quality speaker systems
- In the early 2000s, better file **compression** formats reduced the size of audio files without an effect on the sound quality. MP4/AAC files are used by iTunes and many other online music platforms

- These files are still compressed and thus are not as good as CD quality, but many listeners are willing to make the trade-off considering digital music's convenience and portability.

COMPARING THE BIT RATE OF MP3 AND CD AUDIO

- The **bit rate** of CD audio is just over 1411kbps (kilobits per second)
- MP3 bit rates range from 96kbps to 320kbps
- This shows the amount of compression that has taken place in comparison to CD audio.

Advantages	Disadvantages
■ Portable and easy to share; you can attach compressed digital audio file to an email or share using cloud services, due to its small file size ■ Easy to buy or stream albums – this can be done at the push of a button.	■ Lossy formats; this is when some audio data is lost while being encoded. This can cause issues with the stereo field on a recording and mask effects, whilst also introducing unwanted artefacts onto the track ■ Lack of 'physical' product and album artwork ■ Digital data is easy to copy and thus copied or shared audio files can affect a musician's income.

- Online **streaming** services such as YouTube and Spotify have gained increasing popularity in recent years, and at the time of writing, are the key way that music is listened to
- This has had an impact on other areas of the music business, with artists receiving less money for streaming music than previously would have been the case through singles and album sales
- These services stream compressed audio, so the quality is not as good as for CD audio. However, as with MP3 files, many listeners are willing to make the trade-off considering digital music's convenience and portability, and many can't hear the difference

ONLINE STREAMING

- As an example, at the time of writing, Spotify's iPhone app streams at a 'normal' bit rate of 96kbps and a 'high' bit rate at 160kbps. It also offers an 'extreme' bit rate of 320kbps

- It also matters what equipment you're listening to the music on, as well as where you're listening. 96kbps might sound fine when listening through earbuds on the bus, but will sound poorer on a high-quality stereo system

- Producers are now mixing and mastering with online streaming in mind. Many online streaming services add extra processing to music, for example volume normalisation and limiting.

Turn to page 35 to learn more about the impact of dynamic processing as part of online streaming.

As you develop your skills in the practical tasks, you are also developing your critical and analytical listening skills – in fact, every time you listen to a piece of music you are doing this!

This section concisely covers the styles you need to know for your AS Level in terms of:

- A brief outline of the style: dates, instruments and influences
- Main artists and their significant recordings
- The features of each style's technology and production.

It is useful to think of Music Technology as being divided up into five 'eras'.

c. 1930–1963	**Direct to tape mono recording**	■ Recordings often feature hiss due to the poor **signal-to-noise ratio** ■ Indistinct balance and **EQ** due to the limited number of tracks.
c. 1964–1969	**Early multitrack recording**	■ The balance could still be poor because of restricted tracks, especially on drums ■ A time of experimentation with effects.
c. 1969–1995	**Large-scale analogue multitrack**	■ Increased clarity of parts ■ More tracks meaning further chances to experiment and record with multiple microphones.
c. 1980–present day	**Digital recording and sequencing**	■ Repetitive loops in sequenced parts ■ Less hiss in digital recording ■ Brighter mixes.
c. 1996–present day	**Digital audio workstations (DAW) and emerging technologies**	■ Lots of editing ■ Flawless performances ■ Flex time and pitch/Auto-Tune.

Jazz

The term 'jazz' covers a wide range of styles originating in the American Deep South in cities such as New Orleans and St. Louis around the turn of the 20th century. As it developed, it took several diverse twists, reinventing itself along the way.

Most jazz styles share the common features listed below:

- Originally written and performed mainly by African-Americans
- Improvisation and soloing on lead instruments with highly-accomplished technical musicianship; saxophone and trumpet in particular but other brass instruments too
- Other solo instruments include piano, guitar, clarinet, trombone, flute and vibraphone
- Vocals used in some styles, but others mostly instrumental.

Big band and swing

Dates	1930s and 1940s
Instrumentation	**Big band: rhythm section** of drums, upright (acoustic or double) bass, piano and/or guitar, sometimes banjo. Top-line instruments of large brass and reed section: trumpets, cornets, trombones, saxophones, clarinets. Some use of vocals (female and male), but mostly instrumental. **Jazz combo:** same rhythm section as big band, but fewer top-line instruments.
Influences	■ Ragtime ■ New Orleans Jazz ■ Blues ■ Brass band ■ Popular song/Tin Pan Alley ■ Vaudeville.

Main artists

- Duke Ellington: 'Mood Indigo' (1931), 'Caravan' (1937), 'Satin Doll' (1953)
- Count Basie: 'One O'Clock Jump' (1937), 'Jumpin' At The Woodside' (1938)
- Louis Armstrong: 'Memories Of You' (1930), 'When The Saints Go Marching In' (1938)
- Cab Calloway: 'Minnie The Moocher' (1931), 'Reefer Man' (1933)
- Benny Goodman: 'Sometimes I'm Happy' (1935), 'Stompin' At The Savoy' (1935)
- Glenn Miller: 'In the Mood' (1940), 'Chattanooga Choo Choo' (1942)
- Coleman Hawkins: 'Body and Soul' (1939)
- Billie Holiday: 'Summertime' (1936), 'Strange Fruit' (1939), 'Fine and Mellow' (1939)
- Ella Fitzgerald: '(If You Can't Sing It) You'll Have To Swing It' (1936), 'A-Tisket, A-Tasket' (1938).

Technology and production

- The 1930s saw improvements in music production, and the availability of recorded music for public consumption
- Microphone technology developed and ultimately led to dynamic and **condenser microphones**, with better **frequency** and dynamic responses, along with **valve** amplification
- Commercial success of gramophone players for playback of 78 RPM records (although these did not reproduce a very wide frequency range)
- The quality was also limited by recording medium (direct to disc)
- Recording remained a **capture** of live performances only, though spot-miking techniques started to be used
- Skill of the musicians in producing a balanced sound was important in creating clear recordings
- Development of radio for public broadcast.

Stride piano	Boogie woogie
Piano style using alternating bass notes and chords in the left hand to create the pulse, with melodic improvisation in the right hand.	Piano with left hand playing heavily **swung** quaver patterns, alternating between a walking scalic pattern on the beats and octave root notes on the off-beats. The right hand plays melodies and improvises as in stride.

JAZZ

Gypsy jazz

Dates	1930s, remained popular through the 1940s into the 1950s.
Instrumentation	Acoustic steel strung guitars, double bass, violin, sometimes piano, occasionally vocals with frenetic soloing shared between instruments.
Influences	▪ Swing ▪ Music Hall/musical theatre ▪ Gypsy and Eastern European folk.

Main artists

- Django Reinhardt and his Quintette du Hot Club de France: 'Minor Swing' (1937), 'Nuages' (1940), 'Swing 42' (1941)
- Stèphane Grappelli – violinist who played with Reinhardt.

Bebop, cool jazz and free jazz

	Bebop	Cool jazz	Free jazz
Dates	Early 1940s to early 1950s.	Late 1940s into the 1960s.	Late 1950s to late 1960s.
Instrumen-tation	Small jazz **combos**, normally instrumental with no vocals.		
Influences	▪ Swing ▪ Big band.	▪ Blues ▪ Bebop ▪ Swing.	▪ Bebop ▪ Cool jazz ▪ Swing.
Artists	Coleman Hawkins Charlie Parker Dizzy Gillespie Thelonious Monk	Miles Davis Gerry Mulligan Dave Brubeck Bill Evans	Ornette Coleman John Coltrane Charles Mingus Archie Shepp Sun Ra

Key facts

- Although influential, bebop didn't have widespread appeal or commercial success
- It was a difficult musician's music – hard to play and hard to listen to as casual enjoyment
- In the 1950s and into the 1960s, the hard bop sound developed with R&B influences
- The 'beat generation' identified with the artistry and intellectual quality of bebop. Cool jazz shared some of this musical adventurousness, but had more spacious arrangements and slower tempos
- Free jazz was, in many cases, difficult and challenging to the listener, with loose arrangements, extensive improvisation and a lack of constraints or musical boundaries, resulting in a varied body of work.

Technology and production

- Early recordings similar to other jazz recordings of the same era in the 1940s
- During the 1950s, the use of tape recorders, improvements in microphones and **amplification/mixing desks,** and the introduction of vinyl records led to very fine recordings of live jazz ensembles
- Cool jazz demonstrated clearer and more precise recordings of individual instruments, using improved microphone and recording technology, and close or spot mic techniques
- There are some excellent recordings from the 1950s and 1960s, that still act as a benchmark for recording quality, e.g. Miles Davis's *Kind Of Blue*
- Live ensemble performances and little use of multitrack.

Latin jazz

- In the 1960s, American jazz players collaborated with Brazilian, Cuban and other Latin American musicians – Stan Getz and Dizzy Gillespie in particular
- Percussion parts played typical Latin rhythms, influenced by popular dance styles like samba, salsa and bossa nova
- Instruments were sometimes based on jazz **combos,** but also used horn sections, Latin percussion (for example, congas, bongos and cowbells) with vocals
- Important artists include João and Astrud Gilberto, Tito Puente and Buena Vista Social Club.

Jazz fusion

- As pop became more adventurous and explored new technologies in the later part of the 1960s and into the 1970s, jazz musicians started to experiment with fusing new pop styles using improvisation and jazz techniques/approaches
- Jazz-funk and jazz-rock became identifiable styles, but many other styles used jazz influences in less obvious ways
- Snarky Puppy is a band formed in 2004 that consists of around 40 players, fusing jazz with rock and funk.

Blues

Dates	Origins in late 1800s/early 1900s.
Instrumentation	**Early acoustic blues**: vocals (predominantly male), acoustic guitar, piano, harmonica, some backing vocals.
	Electric blues: vocals (usually male), electric guitar, electric or acoustic bass, drums, piano, harmonica, backing vocals.
	Small ensembles, with either electric guitar or piano featured as the main harmony and solo instrument. Larger ensembles were sometimes used, particularly from the 1960s onwards with more guitars, electric organ, brass sections or solo sax/trumpet.
Influences	■ African-American work songs
	■ Ragtime
	■ Spirituals
	■ European and African folk.

Key facts

- Began as an evolution from African-American folk music, including a large repertoire of songs previously used as work and community songs
- Origins in the rural southern United States around the Mississippi Delta, played by black plantation workers and farm hands on acoustic instruments

- Migration to the cities led to the evolution of electric blues in the 1940s and into the 1950s – based in cities such as Chicago, New Orleans, St. Louis, Memphis; also on the West Coast in Los Angeles
- Little commercial success in the early years – 1930s recordings classed as race music by the big record companies and not marketed to white audiences
- Independent record companies emerged in the 1940s and started releasing and promoting blues music
- The popularity of blues with its original audience of African-Americans declined in the 1960s as other styles emerged, but many blues performers like B.B. King and John Lee Hooker gained recognition on the world stage
- Melancholy lyrical themes of relationship and money problems, oppression and everyday life, but with some spiritual and religious themes
- Blues guitarists had an influence on the 1960s emerging rock sound.

Early acoustic blues

Main artists

- Robert Johnson: 'Cross Road Blues' (1936)
- John Lee Hooker: 'Boogie Chillen'' (1948), 'Boom Boom' (1962)
- Lead Belly: 'The Titanic', 'Midnight Special', 'Cotton Fields', 'Goodnight Irene' (during the mid to late 1930s)
- Tampa Red: 'Black Angel Blues', 'Crying Won't Help You', 'It's Tight Like That' (early to mid-1940s)
- Big Joe Williams: 'Baby, Please Don't Go' (1935)
- Bessie Smith: 'Downhearted Blues' (1923), 'St. Louis Blues' (1925).

Electric blues

Main artists

- Muddy Waters: 'Rollin' Stone' (1950), 'Hoochie Coochie Man' (1954)
- Buddy Guy: *A Man And The Blues* (1967)
- T-Bone Walker: 'Call It Stormy Monday (But Tuesday Is Just As Bad)' (1947), 'Bobby Sox Blues' (1946)
- Howlin' Wolf: 'Smokestack Lightnin'' (1956), 'Spoonful' (1960), 'The Red Rooster' (1962)
- Elmore James: 'Dark And Dreary' (1954), 'Blues Before Sunrise' (1955)
- B.B. King: 'Three O'Clock Blues' (1951), 'Every Day I Have the Blues' (1955), 'The Thrill is Gone' (1970).

Technology and production

- In the post-war era, the move over to tape recording and better quality microphones and **mixing desks** led to better recordings
- Recorded as a live ensemble to allow interaction between performers for improvisation
- Use of the electric guitar and amplification – blues players developed the sound of overdriven guitar, discovering the thicker tone and edge to the sound that made their music more exciting and aggressive
- 20th century blues guitarists developed the slide/bottleneck guitar style.

Independent 1950s record companies

Sun Studio

- Set up in 1950 in Memphis, run by Sam Phillips; as an independent record company, Sun produced music for many of the local artists including blues acts B.B. King and Howlin' Wolf
- Developed new country and rock'n'roll artists like Johnny Cash, Elvis Presley, Carl Perkins, Roy Orbison and Jerry Lee Lewis
- Sam Phillips is particularly associated with the use of slapback tape **delay** as part of the rock'n'roll sound.

Chess Records

- Based in Chicago and set up by the brothers Leonard and Phil Chess at the start of the 1950s, Chess produced most of the big names in blues – including John Lee Hooker, Muddy Waters and Willie Dixon, who was also a bassist and songwriter for the label
- During the 1960s, they adapted to record soul artists such as Fontella Bass.

Atlantic Records

- Atlantic was based in New York and was well known for jazz recordings, but also recorded some blues and R&B acts, notably Ray Charles
- It was an important label for soul music in the 1960s, releasing many Stax recordings, and later became hugely successful, signing Led Zeppelin and Crosby, Stills & Nash.

Rhythm and blues

Dates	Early 1950s to early 1960s.
Instrumentation	Vocals (female and male), backing vocals, drums, bass, guitars, piano, horn sections quite common.
Influences	▪ Blues ▪ Boogie-woogie ▪ Doo-wop ▪ Gospel.

Key facts

- Rhythm and blues was a loose term used by music journalists and record companies to replace the term 'race music' in the 1940s and 1950s
- The term was first used to refer to any music by black artists; the R&B charts were separate from the mainstream charts
- The term has never gone away, with the current usage referring to urban black music styles with influences from soul, hip hop, other electronic music and pop
- R&B forms a clear link between blues and soul music.

Main artists

- Ray Charles: 'Mess Around' (1953), 'Hallelujah I Love Her So' (1955), 'Georgia On My Mind' (1960), 'Hit The Road Jack' (1961), 'One Mint Julep' (1951)
- Ruth Brown: '(Mama) He Treats Your Daughter Mean' (1953), 'Sweet Baby Of Mine' (1956)
- The Drifters: 'Honey Love' (1954), 'There Goes My Baby' (1956), 'Save The Last Dance For Me' (1960), 'Under The Boardwalk' (1964)
- Ben E. King: 'Stand by Me' (1961)
- Sam Cooke: 'You Send Me' (1957), 'Wonderful World', 'Chain Gang' (1960) 'A Change Is Gonna Come' (1964).

Many of the blues and soul artists were also considered R&B artists.

Rock'n'roll

Dates	1950s and early 1960s.
Instrumentation	Vocals (predominantly male), backing vocals, electric guitar, double bass or electric bass, drums, piano; less frequent use of acoustic guitar, harmonica, saxophone and other brass. Ensembles are typically small – vocals, one or two guitars, bass and drums.
Influences	<ul><li>Country</li><li>Blues</li><li>R&B</li><li>Gospel.</li></ul>

Key facts

- Rock'n'roll had widespread popularity and commercial success in the USA and UK, and developed in the urban areas of the southern states of the USA, in cities such as Memphis

- Notion of the pop star, with associated fashion and ownership of the music by the young, reflected a time of change in society

- Increasing prosperity during the 1950s, increasing availability and promotion of music through radio, TV and 7" vinyl singles all played a part in defining youth teen culture

- Predominantly black in origin but widely adopted by white performers; this also helped promote popularity and reflected the increasing acceptance of black people in American society

- Controversial performers gave the music a rebel image, and studios such as Chess Records and Sun Studios played a part in defining the sound

- Lyrics reflected the association with youth–teen life and love, getting and spending money and having a good time; also, boastful lyrics talking of personal success and ability

- Elvis Presley was the first pop superstar – 'the King of rock'n'roll'.

Main artists

- Bill Haley and His Comets: 'Rock Around The Clock' (1954), 'See You Later, Alligator' (1956)

- Little Richard: 'Tutti Frutti' (1957), 'Lucille' (1958)

- Chuck Berry: 'Maybellene' (1955), 'Roll Over Beethoven' (1956), 'Rock And Roll Music' (1957), 'Johnny B. Goode' (1958)
- Elvis Presley: 'Hound Dog' (1956), 'All Shook Up', 'Jailhouse Rock' (1957)
- Jerry Lee Lewis: 'Whole Lotta Shakin' Goin' On', 'Great Balls of Fire' (1957)
- Bo Diddley: 'Bo Diddley', 'I'm A Man' (1956), 'Diddy Wah Diddy' (1957)
- Cliff Richard: 'Move It' (1958) – generally considered the first UK rock'n'roll recording.

Technology and production

- Live recordings direct to tape – mixing done 'on the fly'
- **Capture** of instruments often compromised by poor **frequency** reproduction due to mic positioning and **spill**
- No multi-mic setups on drums used, often just one overhead mic
- Loud guitars and drums were creating new challenges for recording engineers – recording levels were becoming louder through the desk and onto tape, leading to altered sound through driving pre-amps hard and **tape saturation**
- Vocals were sometimes added later (overdubbed) to increase clarity and minimise spill
- Early three-track recorders were used in the 1950s. Alternatively, overdub was achieved using two tape recorders and mixing instrumentals already recorded with the vocal recording
- Some very good recordings were achieved despite the limitations of the recording process – microphones, desks, processing and tape recorders were capable of reproducing high quality results comparable with more modern equipment
- The music was released on vinyl which had superseded 78 RPM records. Vinyl provided an improvement in quality with wider frequency reproduction and better dynamic range
- Slapback **delay** was used on vocals and guitar

For more about slapback delay, turn to page 45.

- Use of echo chambers
- Sound of the electric guitar is crucial in this music – use of overdriven **valve amplifiers** hinting at the full-blown sound of rock guitar that would soon become popular.

For more about how **valve amplifiers** are used to create **distortion**, turn to page 49.

ROCKABILLY

Rockabilly was the name given to rock'n'roll performed by white singers with a country influence. Artists such as Roy Orbison, Eddy Cochran, Carl Perkins and Buddy Holly released rockabilly music in the mid-1950s to early 1960s.

Britain in the 1960s

Key facts

- After the explosion of youth culture and interest in music that accompanied rock'n'roll in the 1950s, young bands started forming throughout the USA and in Britain
- Influences came from American rock'n'roll, R&B, early soul and Motown, but the music quickly evolved in different directions
- New musical styles that emerged were broadly classed as rock; in Britain, songs with strong melodies, harmonies and more complex forms and arrangements than rock'n'roll or R&B were typical (The Beatles, The Animals, The Hollies, The Zombies)
- In the US, a strong folk-rock or country-rock tradition took shape (Bob Dylan, Neil Young, The Beach Boys, Janis Joplin, Joni Mitchell)

For more on folk and country music, turn to page 111.

- Bands with a harder edge to their sound also emerged, such as The Rolling Stones, The Kinks and The Who. These bands influenced the development of heavy metal in the 1970s
- Later in the decade, psychedelic rock bands emerged such as Pink Floyd and The Small Faces. These bands had a big influence on the progressive rock of the 1970s

- It's hard to categorise a lot of the groups in this era, since they made use of so many influences: blues, R&B, gospel, soul, country, folk, rock'n'roll and even classical music
- Many groups also experimented with different styles at various stages of their career, or regularly mixed up soft ballads with harder, R&B-influenced music.

For more about commercial pop styles and their origins from the 1960s to present day, turn to page 114.

Main artists

- The Beatles, The Rolling Stones and The Who (see profiles)
- The Kinks: 'You Really Got Me' (1964), 'Waterloo Sunset' (1967)
- The Small Faces: 'Itchycoo Park' (1967), *Ogdens' Nut Gone Flake*, 'Lazy Sunday' (1968)
- The Animals: 'House Of The Rising Sun' (1964), 'We Gotta Get Out Of This Place' (1965)
- The Hollies: 'He Ain't Heavy, He's My Brother' (1969), 'The Air That I Breathe' (1974)
- The Spencer Davis Group: 'Keep On Running' (1965), 'Gimme Some Lovin'' (1966)
- The Yardbirds: 'Heart Full Of Soul', *For Your Love* (1965)
- The Moody Blues: 'Nights In White Satin' (1967), 'Question' (1970).

The Beatles

Dates	1960-1970
Instrumentation	Vocals (lead shared by John Lennon and Paul McCartney; George Harrison and Ringo Starr also sang lead on some songs), backing vocals from all band members, drums, bass, electric guitar, acoustic guitar, 12-string acoustic guitar, piano, percussion; ensembles became more diverse to include orchestral sections, electronic keyboards and experimental studio sounds.

Key facts

- Perhaps the single most influential band in the story of popular music, the band formed in their home town of Liverpool

- They were the first band to achieve worldwide recognition, with huge international sales of all their work continuing today
- Their more diverse, later sound had strong elements of psychedelic rock, including diverse instrumentation and the use of sonic experimentation – recording ambient sound to mix with the music, reverse tape recordings, use of extreme **reverb** and **delay** settings, and effects such as phasing and flange.

Please Please Me (1963)

- Influenced by R&B and the American popular sound, it was essentially **captured** as live performances of their live set, recorded to two-track tape with instruments on one track and vocals on the other, then mixed to **mono**.

With The Beatles (1963)

- Marked the start of the British Invasion with straight-up rock/pop and more diverse instrumentation that included a range of percussion, Hammond organ and harmonica
- Sound-on-sound **overdubbing** and double-tracked vocals were used, and the album was released in mono and stereo; the stereo version featuring polarised **panning** is unconventional by modern standards.

A Hard Day's Night (1964)

- The film soundtrack featured some instrumentals and folk-influenced songs
- Recorded onto four-track multitrack and mixed in both mono and stereo.

Beatles For Sale (1964)

- 'Eight Days A Week' was recorded in several different takes; points to early studio experimentation and includes a fade-in at the start.

Help! (1965)

- Another film soundtrack that included more overdubs and orchestral instruments featured on 'Yesterday' and 'You've Got To Hide Your Love Away'.

Rubber Soul (1965)

- Combined some more diverse and unusual approaches, using a sitar on 'Norwegian Wood' and with folk influences
- Included unconventional treatments of piano including sped-up recordings and heavy **compression**.

Revolver (1966)

- Continued the experimentation with classical elements, notably on 'Eleanor Rigby' with the stark string arrangement

- Emergence of psychedelic influence; 'Tomorrow Never Knows' features tape loops, vocal effects and reverse guitar
- The first album to use automatic double tracking.

Sgt. Pepper's Lonely Hearts Club Band (1967)

- Songs use a story-based narrative, touching on a wide range of themes and views on life ('concept album')
- Lots of **overdubbing**, with experiments using varied tape speed, playing vocals and guitars through a Leslie speaker, using flanging, **wah wah** and fuzz and the use of the Mellotron.

Magical Mystery Tour (1967)

- The music from the film of the same name was released as an extended play six-track set
- The songs continued the psychedelic sound of *Sgt. Pepper's*, with 'I Am The Walrus' being a good example of experimentation, with its effects and sound collages.

The Beatles (The White Album) (1968)

- Continued the psychedelic themes of *Sgt. Pepper's Lonely Hearts Club Band*, with a wide range of styles from typical rock/pop to acoustic offerings and music-hall influences
- Recorded on eight-track tape and produced many notable songs such as 'Dear Prudence', 'Let It Be', 'Blackbird' and 'While My Guitar Gently Weeps' (featuring Eric Clapton).

Yellow Submarine (1969)

- Another film soundtrack; quite a few of the songs were re-worked from earlier versions, and the second side was an orchestral score composed by The Beatles' producer George Martin.

Abbey Road (1969)

- The last album recorded before the band split, featuring hits 'Something', 'Come Together' and 'Here Comes The Sun'
- Recorded on eight-track, making use of the Moog synthesiser.

Let It Be (1970)

- Recording took place before Abbey Road; released after the band's split
- Generally seen as the weakest album, despite hits 'Let It Be', 'The Long and Winding Road' and 'Get Back'.

The Rolling Stones

Dates	Mid to late 1960s; continued to write, record and perform successfully throughout the 1980s and remain active today.
Instrumentation	Vocals, backing vocals, electric guitar, bass, drums, percussion; piano/keyboards, strings and horns on occasion.

Key facts

- Rivals to The Beatles for popularity in the mid to late 1960s
- Part of the British Invasion that enjoyed popularity in the USA in the mid to late 1960s
- Continued to write, record and perform successfully throughout the 1970s and 1980s, remaining active today.

Main releases

Successful albums include:

Their Satanic Majesties Request (1967), *Beggers Banquet* (1968), *Let It Bleed* (1969), *Sticky Fingers* (1971), *Exile On Main Street* (1972), *Goat's Head Soup* (1973), *It's Only Rock 'n' Roll* (1974), *Black and Blue* (1976), *Some Girls* (1978), *Emotional Rescue* (1980), *Tattoo You* (1981).

Successful singles include:

- 'It's All Over Now' (1964)
- '(I Can't Get No) Satisfaction', 'Get Off Of My Cloud' (1965)
- 'Let's Spend The Night Together' (1967)
- 'Jumpin' Jack Flash' (1968)
- 'Honky Tonk Women' (1969)
- 'Brown Sugar' (1971)
- 'Miss You' (1978).

The Who

Dates	Initially 1964-1983 with reunions running to present day.
Instrumentation	Vocals, backing vocals, guitar, bass, drums, percussion; synthesiser and keyboards, horns.

Key facts

- Mod culture – a youth sub-culture who wore sharp suits and rode scooters
- Pete Townshend known for 'windmill' guitar playing style
- The band used synthesisers extensively in the early 1970s
- High energy, aggressive performers who smashed up guitars and drum kits in their act
- Their mainstream music sometimes called 'power pop'.

Main releases

Successful albums include:

My Generation (1965), *A Quick One* (1966), *The Who Sell Out* (1967), *Tommy* (1969), *Who's Next* (1971) and *Quadrophenia* (1973)

Successful singles include:

- 'My Generation' (1965)
- 'I Can See For Miles' (1967)
- 'Pinball Wizard' (1969)
- 'Substitute' (1970).

Rock and pop in the 1970s

Psychedelic rock

Dates	Later part of the 1960s and early 1970s.
Instrumentation	Classic rock band line-up with guitars, drums, bass and often keyboards; vocals and backing vocals; unusual instruments such as sitar, mandolin, dulcimer and the Mellotron keyboard, an early sampler.
Influences	- UK rock - Folk rock - Experimental music such as Musique Concrète.

Key facts

- Linked to the beat generation culture around Los Angeles and San Francisco, and the free festivals like Woodstock in the USA and the Isle of Wight festival in the UK

- The use of mind-altering drugs led to many of the musical experiments in psychedelic rock
- Lyrical themes are surreal, fairy tale or mystical, and a number of bands released concept albums
- Little attempt to produce commercial, radio-friendly, three-minute pop songs.

Main artists

- The Grateful Dead: *The Grateful Dead* (1967)
- Country Joe and the Fish: *Electric Music For The Mind And Body* (1967)
- The Doors: *The Doors* (1967)
- Frank Zappa: *Freak Out!* (1966)
- Captain Beefheart: *Trout Mask Replica* (1969)
- Tangerine Dream: *Electronic Meditation* (1970)
- Hawkwind: *Hawkwind* (1970), 'Silver Machine' (1972)
- Gong: *Flying Teapot* (1973).

Many bands had periods or just some songs where the psychedelic influence was evident:

- The Beatles: 'Day Tripper' (1965), 'Lucy In The Sky With Diamonds', 'I Am The Walrus' (1967)
- The Who: 'I Can See For Miles' (1967)
- The Rolling Stones: 'Paint It Black' (1966)
- The Small Faces: *Ogdens' Nut Gone Flake* (1968)
- Pink Floyd: early albums, listed under *Progressive rock*, page 89
- Jimi Hendrix: see *Heavy rock*, page 91.

Technology and production

- Guitar sounds use plenty of processing – **distortion**, feedback, fuzz, **phaser**, echo/delay, Leslie speaker
- Mellotron used to produce choir, flute and string sounds often as **pads** or drones
- Large amounts of **reverb** and **delay** used to produce unreal-sounding textures
- Could be used on any part of the mix such as vocals, guitars, keyboards, or solo instruments like flute
- Phasers and **flangers** popular for similar reasons
- Synthesisers used for capability to produce unusual sounds
- Tape loops and ambient recordings used to add strange non-musical sounds and textures.

Progressive rock

Dates	Late 1960s to mid-1970s.
Instrumentation	Drums, bass, guitar, keyboards – synthesisers, electric organ and electric piano, vocals and backing vocals; sometimes strings, horns and world instruments.
Influences	■ UK rock of The Beatles, The Who and The Kinks ■ The Velvet Underground and psychedelic rock ■ Jazz ■ World music ■ Classical.

Key facts

- Began alongside or as part of the psychedelic rock scene; by the end of the 1970s, the music was seen as outdated and stale
- Focus on albums based on themes or a concept rather than singles for commercial success
- Genesis's 1974 album *The Lamb Lies Down* was a concept album based on a mythical folk tale, seen as adventurous and experimental for its musical forms and use of electronics; Brian Eno contributed synthesiser parts
- Many bands evolved to have a more commercial sound and chart success in the 1980s, including Pink Floyd, Yes and Genesis; Pink Floyd had international success with *Dark Side Of The Moon*.

Main artists

- Pink Floyd: *The Piper At The Gates Of Dawn* (1967), *Dark Side Of The Moon* (1973), *The Wall* (1979)
- King Crimson: *In The Court Of The Crimson King* (1969)
- Yes: *Close To The Edge* (1972)
- Genesis: *Trespass* (1970), *Nursery Cryme* (1971), *Selling England By The Pound* (1973), *The Lamb Lies Down On Broadway (1974)*
- Jethro Tull: *Aqualung* (1971)
- Soft Machine: *Volume Two* (1969)
- The Moody Blues: *Days Of Future Passed* (1967)
- Emerson, Lake & Palmer: *Tarkus* (1971).

Like psychedelic rock, some bands were not exclusively progressive rock and demonstrated a variety of influences.

Technology and production

- Production tried to achieve the highest technical excellence possible – lush **reverbs**, **delays** and expensive-sounding layered recordings
- Guitar sounds ranged from clean sounds, use of effects like **chorus**, **flanger** and **phaser** to full-on heavy-rock **distortion** and fuzz
- Synthesisers were often used for solo work rather than sound effects and played an important role
- The Moog and ARP were fairly new instruments but were used extensively alongside other electronic keyboards such as the electric organ and electric piano.

Heavy rock

Dates	Late 1960s to mid-1980s, with influences to present day.
Instrumentation	Many bands use two guitarists, drums, bass, vocals (usually male), keyboards (fairly common, though not often in a very prominent role).
Influences	<ul><li>Blues</li><li>R&B</li><li>Progressive rock</li><li>British blues</li><li>Psychedelic rock.</li></ul>

Key facts

- The development of the electric guitar was central to heavy rock, blues and rock'n'roll guitarists such as John Lee Hooker, Muddy Waters, B.B. King and Chuck Berry; they helped to make the electric guitar a prominent centrepiece to the sound of popular music, and the distorted tone of the guitar characterises heavy rock
- Jimi Hendrix's music fused diverse elements of funk, soul, psychedelia and jazz with his heavily blues-fuelled playing. He was also a virtuosic electric guitarist whose technique and use of effects drove forward the development of the instrument

- Other 1960s guitarists took the blues style and made it harder and heavier; in particular, Eric Clapton (Cream) and Pete Townshend (The Who), but the next crop of bands to really develop the style included Led Zeppelin and Deep Purple in the early 1970s

- Stage acts were extravagant, long and loud. The image was about rebellion, the freedom to be individual and 'live hard, die young'

- Bands such as Kiss, Queen, Thin Lizzy, Alice Cooper and Aerosmith were all successful in the UK and USA in the first half of the 1970s, and adopted the influence of the sound while staying in a slightly more pop-oriented vein

- In Canada, Rush's first three albums were very much in the heavy-rock style, and female-led group Heart proved that not all heavy rock was male-oriented

- By the mid-1970s, Deep Purple had split up and though Zeppelin's tours were outselling The Rolling Stones, heavy rock was becoming unfashionable

- Newer bands emerging in the late 1970s and early 1980s had less of a blues influence, usually referred to as heavy metal

- Examples at this time were Motörhead – a faster, punk-influenced version of heavy rock; and the new wave of British bands that followed at the end of the 1970s, led by Iron Maiden, Saxon and Def Leppard, and Metallica and Megadeth in the USA

- At the end of the 1970s, Van Halen emerged in the USA and AC/DC from Australia

- Both enjoyed massive worldwide success, with Eddie Van Halen guesting on guitar for Michael Jackson's single 'Thriller', and his own single 'Jump' reaching number one in 1984

- AC/DC released the massively successful *Highway To Hell* in 1979 and followed it with *Back In Black* in 1980

- The influence of heavy rock has continued since the 1980s, though only a few of the original bands still remain active – including Aerosmith, Bon Jovi and Van Halen

- Newer styles such as grunge and metal sub-genres are direct descendants of the 1960s and 1980s heavy rock artists.

Main artists

- Jimi Hendrix: 'Hey Joe' (1965), 'Purple Haze' (1967), *Are You Experienced* (1967), *Axis: Bold As Love* (1967), *Electric Ladyland* (1968), 'Voodoo Chile' (1968), 'All Along The Watchtower' (1968)

- Led Zeppelin released the albums *Led Zeppelin I, II, III and IV* from 1969 to 1971 followed by four more in the 1970s. Well-known songs include 'Whole Lotta Love' (1969), 'Black Dog', 'Rock and Roll', 'Stairway To Heaven' (1971), 'Kashmir' (1975)

- Deep Purple: 'Black Night' (1970), 'Smoke On The Water' (1972), 'Woman From Tokyo' (1973)
- Black Sabbath: 'Paranoid' (1970), *Sabbath Bloody Sabbath* (1973)
- Motörhead: *Motörhead* (1977), *Ace Of Spades* (1980)
- Iron Maiden: 'The Trooper' (1983), 'Two Minutes To Midnight' (1984)
- Saxon: 'Motorcycle Man' (1980), *Wheels Of Steel* (1980), *Princess Of The Night* (1981)
- Def Leppard: 'Bringin' On The Heartbreak' (1981), 'Rock Of Ages' (1983).

Bands from the USA included Metallica, Megadeth, Bon Jovi and Van Halen.

Technology and production

- **Distortion**, **valve** amp sound, and effects used to create a massive guitar sound
- Use of effects: fuzz, **wah wah** and **phaser**
- Use of feedback and finger tapping
- Thick and heavy drums and bass
- Fairly large, obvious **reverbs**.

Glam rock

Dates	1970-1976.
Instrumentation	Vocals (predominantly male) and backing vocals; guitar, bass, drums, keyboards, percussion; sometimes with horns.
Influences	<ul><li>Rock and roll</li><li>Heavy rock</li><li>Psychedelic rock</li><li>1960s pop.</li></ul>

Key facts

- While some glam was intentionally 'disposable', commercial, shallow pop music, other artists had a deeper and more 'arty' approach (David Bowie, Bryan Ferry/Roxy Music)
- Many glam artists were deliberately androgynous

- Lyrics tended to be light and stayed away from controversial themes, although were often sexually suggestive
- Performers were famous for their 'glitzy' delivery: make-up, sparkly costumes and high-heeled boots with larger-than-life stage personas/alter-egos
- Elton John, Queen and Rod Stewart were glam influenced artists who also produced music beyond the style
- David Bowie was an important figure in shaping glam; he reinvented himself throughout his long career spanning the 1970s, 1980s and 1990s, with albums released up until his death in 2016
- Roxy Music only made a few albums at the start of the 1970s and had a strong experimental element through the synthesiser work of Brian Eno, use of the saxophone, oboe and violin. Brian Ferry continued as a solo artist and maintained a successful career throughout the 1970s and 1980s.

Main artists

- T. Rex/Marc Bolan: 'Get It On' (1970), 'Jeepster' (1971), 'Metal Guru' (1972)
- Slade: 'Cum On Feel The Noize', 'Mama Weer All Crazee Now' (1972), 'Merry Xmas Everybody' (1973)
- The Sweet: 'Blockbuster' (1973), 'Ballroom Blitz' (1975)
- David Bowie: 'Space Oddity' (1969), 'Starman' (1972), 'Life On Mars?' (1973)
- Bryan Ferry/Roxy Music: 'Virginia Plain' (1972), 'The 'In' Crowd' (1974)
- Roy Wood/Wizzard: 'See My Baby Jive', 'I Wish It Could Be Christmas Everyday' (1973)
- Mott the Hoople: 'All The Young Dudes' (1972), 'Roll Away The Stone' (1973)
- Suzi Quatro: 'Can The Can' (1973), 'Devil Gate Drive' (1974).

Technology and production

- Similar to other early 1970s rock productions
- Guitar sounds based on **distortion**, fuzz and powerful amplification
- Multitrack recording giving a clear and big sound
- Some use of synthesisers and effects for experimental sounds
- Natural or plate **reverbs**
- Tape echo.

Punk and new wave

Punk

Dates	Mid-1970s to early 1980s; 1977 was key.
Instrumentation	Vocals (mainly male), electric guitar, bass and drums; keyboards used by some bands.
Influences	■ Rock'n'roll ■ Hard rock: The Who and The Velvet Underground ■ Early 1960s pop.

Key facts

- Reaction against the excesses of technical, highly produced progressive rock; the similarly highly polished disco and 1970s pop; and the 'serious' attitude of heavy rock
- Aggressive, anti-establishment, disposable music for the people
- Lyrics featuring social and political commentary and displaying dissatisfaction with the establishment. This was in light of social unrest in the UK due to high unemployment and the battle between unions and government over working conditions and the future of nationalised industries
- Several bands or songs were banned from radio and TV play
- Many bands supported political movements such as The Anti-Nazi League and Rock Against Racism
- Chaotic dancing – pogoing and spitting was common amongst fans at gigs
- Equipment and venues often got smashed up at gigs
- Fashion was important – custom-made clothing covered with zips and safety pins, lots of black, kilts and tartan. Safety pins were also worn as jewellery/ piercings
- Hairstyles included the Mohican, often spiked up and dyed bright colours.

Main artists

- Sex Pistols: 'Anarchy In The UK' (1976), 'God Save The Queen', 'Pretty Vacant' (1977), 'Something Else' (1978)
- The Clash: 'White Riot' (1977), 'Clash City Rockers', 'White Man In Hammersmith Palais', 'Tommy Gun' (1978), 'I Fought The Law', 'London Calling' (1979), 'Bankrobber' (1980), 'Rock The Casbah' (1982)

- The Stranglers: 'Peaches', 'No More Heroes' (1977)
- The Jam: 'The Eton Rifles' (1979), 'Going Underground' (1980)
- The Buzzcocks: 'Ever Fallen In Love (With Someone You Shouldn't Have)' (1978)
- Stiff Little Fingers: 'At The Edge' (1979)
- The Undertones: 'Teenage Kicks' (1978), 'Jimmy Jimmy' (1979)
- The Damned: 'Neat Neat Neat' (1977), 'Love Song' (1979)
- The Ruts: 'In A Rut' (1978), 'Babylon's Burning' (1979)
- Siouxsie and the Banshees: 'Hong Kong Garden' (1978), 'Happy House' (1980).

Punk acts from the USA included the Ramones and the Patti Smith Group.

Technology and production

- DIY production ethic; used independent small studios to create a simple, raw unprocessed sound
- No clever production tricks
- Guitar sounds are often distorted, though quite thin and harsh compared to the full tones of heavy-rock **distortion** and fuzz
- Effects were still used, but producers avoided the polished sound of disco and pop of the era; there was no 'spacey', psychedelic use of effects like **delay** and flanging, and no lush **reverbs**.

New wave

Dates	Late 1970s to early 1980s.
Instrumentation	Vocals (male and female), backing vocals, guitar, drums, percussion, bass, keyboards.
Influences	<ul><li>Punk</li><li>Hard rock</li><li>Reggae</li><li>Funk.</li></ul>

Key facts

- Gained popularity as punk's brief explosion came to an end; many new wave bands and artists later went on to have successful careers as pop artists

- CBGBs club in New York was an important venue, with bands like Blondie, New York Dolls and Talking Heads playing and evolving their sound there alongside the punk sounds of the Ramones

- Like punk, new wave had a strong independence from the establishment, which included the major record companies as well as the government

- Lyrics dealt with social and political issues – there were many clever lyricists such as Ian Dury and Elvis Costello – as well as more conventional pop themes

- Many of the British new wave bands did not gain success in the USA, although The Police, The Pretenders and Elvis Costello had moderate chart popularity with a few songs

- Bands like Joy Division, The Cure and The Psychedelic Furs emerged towards the end of new wave, and formed a bridge between punk, new wave, the synth pop or new romantic sound and the indie rock sound that emerged during the 1980s.

Main artists

- Elvis Costello and the Attractions: 'Watching The Detectives' (1977), '(I Don't Want To Go To) Chelsea', 'Pump It Up' (1978)

- Ian Dury and the Blockheads: 'Sex and Drugs and Rock and Roll' (1977), 'What A Waste', 'Hit Me With Your Rhythm Stick' (1978)

- XTC: 'Making Plans For Nigel' (1979), 'Senses Working Overtime' (1982)

- Squeeze: 'Cool For Cats', 'Up The Junction' (1979)

- The Police: 'Roxanne' (1978), 'Message In A Bottle' (1979), 'Don't Stand So Close to Me' (1980)

- The Pretenders: 'Stop Your Sobbing', 'Brass In Pocket' (1979)

- Blondie: 'Heart Of Glass', 'One Way Or Another' (1978), 'Call Me' (1980)

- Talking Heads: 'Psycho Killer' (1979), 'Once In A Lifetime' (1980).

Other new wave acts included The Cars, Devo, The B-52s and Graham Parker and The Rumour.

Technology and production

- Similar to punk; the aim was to achieve an energetic and unprocessed sound of real musicians

- The productions were still often a bit more polished than punk

- Use of keyboards and more variety in the arrangements often gave more depth to the sound than was usual for punk.

Synth pop

Dates	Mid-1970s and 1980s.
Instrumentation	Drum machines, synthesisers, vocals and backing vocals; guitars and bass sometimes used, especially in later styles.
Influences	■ Kraut rock ■ Disco ■ Art rock ■ Glam rock ■ New wave ■ Punk.

Key facts

- Synth pop's early pioneers were German band Kraftwerk, whose mid-1970s hits were based entirely on drum machine and synthesiser ensembles
- They continued to be an influential band throughout the 1980s
- The first English bands started appearing at the very end of the 1970s and were known as New Romantics, offering an alternative to the chaotic sound of punk
- Duran Duran and Eurythmics were two synth pop bands that had extensive careers and commercial success
- Later acts like Pet Shop Boys adopted the electronic sound but made it more pop-friendly, with strong disco influences.

Main artists

- Ultravox: 'Vienna', 'All Stood Still' (1981), 'Reap The Wild Wind' (1982)
- The Human League: 'Love Action (I Believe In Love)', 'Don't You Want Me' (1981)
- Gary Numan/Tubeway Army: 'Are 'Friends' Electric?', 'Cars' (1979)
- Kraftwerk: 'Autobahn' (1975), 'Trans-Europe Express' (1977)
- Tears For Fears: 'Mad World' (1983), 'Shout', 'Everybody Wants To Rule The World' (1985)
- Soft Cell/Marc Almond: 'Tainted Love' (1981), 'Torch' (1982)
- Orchestral Manoeuvres In The Dark: 'Enola Gay' (1980), 'Locomotion' (1984)
- A-ha: 'Take On Me' (1984), 'I've Been Losing You' (1986)

- Eurythmics: 'Sweet Dreams (Are Made of This)' (1983), 'Sisters Are Doin' It For Themselves' (1985), 'Thorn In My Side' (1986)
- Duran Duran: 'Girls On Film' (1981), 'Rio' (1982), 'The Reflex' (1984).

In the late 2000s/early 2010s, there was a resurgence in music influenced by synth pop, sometimes referred to as electro pop.

- La Roux: *La Roux* (2009), *Trouble In Paradise* (2014)
- Hot Chip: 'Ready for the Floor' (2008), 'Over and Over' (2010)
- Dua Lipa: 'New Rules', 'Be The One' (2017), 'One Kiss' (with Calvin Harris) (2018).

Technology and production

- Often moody and reserved, introspective performances; later more pop-oriented with happier, up-beat dance rhythms
- Synthesisers took the role of guitars, bass and harmony parts from earlier rock styles – use of riffs, melodic hooks, chord patterns
- Use of synth **pads** – **sustaining** synth chords playing patterns or harmony lines
- Early drum machines, and **monophonic/polyphonic** analogue synthesisers provided the sonic signature of the music
- Real-time manipulation of **synthesis** settings such as filter cutoff and **LFOs**
- Drum machines had their own built-in sequencers as did some synthesisers, though they were often played from the keyboard
- Stand-alone sequencers also used – the early songs pre-dated **MIDI** so sequencers used an **analogue** system called **CV/gate**
- Return to lush and obvious **reverbs** after punk.

Indie rock

Dates	Early 1980s to present day, but much music from the 1990s.
Instrumentation	Classic rock band line-up with guitars, drums, bass and sometimes keyboards; vocals and backing vocals. Guitar as the main harmony instrument.

Influences	■ UK rock of The Beatles, The Who and The Kinks
	■ The Velvet Underground and psychedelic rock
	■ Punk rock
	■ Funk
	■ House.

Key facts

■ Often reflected earlier British styles; bands like The Kinks, The Who and edgy 1960s and 1970s guitar-based pop

■ Independent of major record companies with a DIY ethic

■ Built a following on the college and university circuit, and a large number of independent, small to medium-sized venues across the UK

■ Many leading indie acts came from Manchester including The Smiths, The Stone Roses and Happy Mondays

■ Scene linked to Happy Mondays, The Haçienda Nightclub and Factory Records became known as Madchester

■ Strong association with the emerging dance and rave scene.

Main artists

■ Pulp: *Different Class* (1995)

■ Elastica: *Elastica* (1995)

■ The Cure: *Pornography* (1982), *Wish* (1992)

■ The Housemartins: 'Happy Hour', 'Caravan Of Love' (1986)

■ Joy Division: *Unknown Pleasures* (1979), 'Love Will Tear Us Apart' (1980)

■ New Order: *Power, Corruption & Lies*, 'Blue Monday' (1983)

■ The Smiths: 'This Charming Man', 'What Difference Does It Make?' (1983), *The Smiths* (1984), 'Heaven Knows I'm Miserable Now', 'William, It Was Really Nothing', *Meat Is Murder* (1985), *The Queen Is Dead* (1986), *Strangeways Here We Come* (1987)

■ Happy Mondays: *Squirrel And G-Man Twenty Four Hour Party People Plastic Face Carnt Smile (White Out)* (1987), *Bummed* (1988), *Pills 'n' Thrills and Bellyaches* (1990)

■ The Stone Roses: *Stone Roses* (1989), 'Fools Gold' (1989), 'One Love' (1992), *Second Coming* (1994)

■ The Wedding Present: *Seamonsters* (1991)

■ Blur: *Leisure* (1991), *Modern Life Is Rubbish* (1993)

■ Suede: 'The Drowners', 'Metal Mickey' (1992), *Suede* (1993)

■ Idlewild: *The Remote Part* (2002).

Technology and production

- Guitar sounds often referred to as jangly – a fairly light tone using picked, **sustained** arpeggios with effects
- Guitar **amplifiers** and effects play a big part in the sound of indie – the light, sustained tone and use of **delays** is common in many bands
- DIY production ethic; low budget recordings based on simple **capture** of live performances.

Factory Records

- Founded in the late 1970s by Tony Wilson
- Earliest signings included Joy Division (later to become New Order after the death of singer Ian Curtis), The Stone Roses and Orchestral Manoeuvres In The Dark
- Wilson also ran The Haçienda nightclub and gig venue, where many indie bands played
- Other prominent bands to emerge from the Manchester area included Inspiral Carpets, James and The Charlatans
- Joy Division and New Order are also significantly different from many indie bands in their sound, using lots of electronic influences, but still share the same independent ethic.

Rough Trade Records

- An independent record distribution network founded by Geoff Travis, handling the nationwide stocking of record shops for many independent labels
- Punk band Stiff Little Fingers released albums on their label along with The Smiths.

Britpop

- Britpop emerged during the 1990s
- It enjoyed much more success in the mainstream, and tended to be more pop-orientated and lighter in its themes than most indie music, with some humour
- Oasis, later Blur, The Verve and Coldplay were important bands on the Britpop scene.

Grunge

- From America, the grunge style of Nirvana and Alice in Chains was becoming influential, and shared the ethos of indie, if not the sound
- Nirvana, Pearl Jam, Soundgarden and Alice in Chains were well-known grunge bands, and the style was commercially successful in early to mid-1990s.

Soul

Dates	Late 1950s to mid-1970s.
Instrumentation	Vocals and backing vocals – male and female vocalists both used; drums, bass, percussion, electric guitar, piano, electric piano, electric organ, horn section (trumpet, saxes and trombone), string section. Large ensembles, including instruments such as drums and guitars being doubled up.
Influences	<ul><li>R&B</li><li>Gospel</li><li>Jazz singers (such as Billie Holliday and Ella Fitzgerald)</li><li>Psychedelic rock (late 1960s).</li></ul>

Key facts

- Originated in the large cities in the southern states of the USA – Detroit, Memphis and Philadelphia, and also from New York on the East Coast
- It was mainly produced by African-Americans, and gained worldwide commercial success and popularity, enduring until the present day
- Lyrical themes relate to love lost or found, as well as partying and having a good time
- Motown records avoided lyrics of a sexual nature due to the desire to stay non-controversial and commercial
- Artists such as James Brown were not afraid to be a bit more direct
- Social issues were also avoided by Motown, despite the background of the black civil rights movement and the Vietnam War, which were both pressing social issues for young Americans in the late 1960s
- Motown's owner Berry Gordy ultimately bowed to the wishes of some of the singers, with Edwin Starr recording 'War (What Is It Good For?)' and Marvin Gaye's album *What's Going On?*

Technology and production

- Early adoption of multitrack tape; four-track then eight-track
- Live recording of a band in a single room; use of DI guitars and basses and acoustic screens for separation

SOUL

- Close mic drum recording with overdubbed vocals
- High quality microphones, models still in use today
- Use of echo chambers and plate **reverbs** such as the EMT 140
- Classic compressors such as Teletronix LA2A – though with fairly gentle settings
- Often high-quality recordings with clear vocals and **frequency** reproduction (including deep bass)
- Stereo mixes with extreme **panning**; unconventional by today's standards
- Electronic instruments: Hammond organ and Fender Rhodes
- Very little use of sound design through **synthesis** or extreme guitar effects – focus instead on the natural sound of the instruments.

Main artists

- Sam Cooke: 'You Send Me' (1957), 'Chain Gang' (1960) 'A Change Is Gonna Come' (1964)
- Wilson Pickett: 'In The Midnight Hour' (1965), 'Mustang Sally' (1966)
- Otis Redding: 'Sitting On The Dock Of The Bay' (1967)
- The Temptations: 'My Girl' (1965), 'Cloud Nine' (1968), 'Papa Was A Rollin' Stone' (1972)
- Stevie Wonder: 'Uptight (Everything's Alright)' (1966), 'Yester-Me, Yester-You, Yesterday' (1968), 'Superstition' (1972)
- Al Green: 'Let's Stay Together' (1972)
- Marvin Gaye: 'How Sweet It Is (To Be Loved By You)' (1964), 'I Heard It Through The Grapevine' (1968), *What's Going On* (1971)
- The Supremes/Diana Ross: 'Where Did Our Love Go' (1964), 'Baby Love' (1964), 'Stop! In The Name Of Love' (1965), 'You Can't Hurry Love' (1965)
- The Jackson 5/Michael Jackson: 'ABC' (1969), 'Never Can Say Goodbye' (1971), 'Ben' (1972)
- The Four Tops: 'I Can't Help Myself', 'It's The Same Old Song' (1965), 'Reach Out, I'll Be There', 'Standing In The Shadows Of Love' (1966)
- Sam & Dave: 'Soul Man' (1967), 'Soul Sister, Brown Sugar' (1969)
- Aretha Franklin: 'Respect', '(You Make Me Feel Like) A Natural Woman' (1967), 'I Say A Little Prayer' (1968)
- James Brown: 'I Got You (I Feel Good)' (1965), 'Say It Loud – I'm Black And I'm Proud' (1968).

Other soul artists include:

- Smokey Robinson: 'The Tears Of A Clown' (1967)
- Lionel Richie: 'Easy' (1977, with the Commodores), 'All Night Long (All Night)' (1984)
- Jackie Wilson: '(Your Love Keeps Lifting Me) Higher And Higher' (1967)
- Sly & The Family Stone: *There's A Riot Goin' On* (1971)
- The Spinners: 'It's A Shame' (1970)
- Dusty Springfield: 'Son Of A Preacher Man' (1968)
- Booker T. & The M.G.'s: 'Green Onions' (1962).

Soul styles and labels

Motown

- Set up in Detroit by songwriter and producer Berry Gordy in the late 1950s
- Independent record company with entire process handled in-house
- Songwriting by various teams or individuals who had to write and record at least five songs a week (Lamont-Dozier-Lamont, Smokey Robinson)
- Recording of the rhythm track took place in three-hour time slots using the house band (The Funk Brothers), with vocals overdubbed separately
- Mixes were reviewed by quality control teams and decisions taken about which songs to release
- Motown developed some of the most successful singers of the 1960s and following decades, including Michael Jackson, Stevie Wonder and Diana Ross.

Stax

- Record label and studio responsible for Memphis soul – generally considered to be rawer and more authentic than Motown, but with less commercial success
- Studio operated in a similar way with a house band – Booker T. & The M.G.'s – provided rhythm tracks for a host of singers and groups, and house writer-producers including Isaac Hayes.

Atlantic

- Larger record label with more links to the big US labels and a working partnership with Stax
- Producer Jerry Wexler worked with Aretha Franklin and Wilson Pickett, and also blue-eyed soul acts from the UK such as Dusty Springfield.

Philadelphia Soul

- Emerged in the late 1960s; polished and smoother sound with big string arrangements
- Producers Gamble and Huff were behind the Philadelphia international label that produced artists such as Jackie Wilson, The O'Jays, The Spinners, The Stylistics and The Three Degrees.

1970s, 1980s and beyond

- Soul became less fashionable in the early part of the 1970s, and songs that were released tended to be smooth ballads from bands such as the Commodores and singers like Barry White
- In the 1980s there was something of a revival in the UK, with bands like Simply Red and Sade drawing on soul influences
- Popular films *The Blues Brothers* and *The Commitments* used soul classics as the soundtrack and part of the storyline.

Disco and funk

Disco

Dates	Mid to late 1970s to mid-1980s.
Instrumentation	Vocals (quite often female but also male), group backing vocals, drums, bass, percussion, guitars, keyboards – particularly electric piano and clavinet, also synthesisers; horn section (using flute, french horn and even tuba in addition to the usual sax, trumpet and trombone); sometimes a string section – generally large ensembles.
Influences	<ul><li>R&B</li><li>Gospel</li><li>Soul (particularly Philadelphia soul)</li><li>Funk</li><li>Latin.</li></ul>

Key facts

- The complexity of the techniques used in the productions was a sign of producers and engineers becoming more involved in the creative possibilities of technology

- It became studio music and pointed the way for other technology-based styles to follow

- Quickly adopted by the pop scene; bands like Boney M., The Bee Gees and Village People had commercial success

- Disco came to represent everything that was bad about pop music for a lot of rock bands and their fans

- Some of the original American bands such as Chic and Earth, Wind & Fire are highly creditable and have had long and successful careers as writers and producers since the disco era

- Donna Summer – 'I Feel Love' (1977), produced by Giorgio Moroder, used a rhythm track completely produced with drum machines and sequenced synthesisers. This was ground-breaking at the time, though now common practice.

Main artists

- Donna Summer: 'Love To Love You Baby' (1975), 'I Feel Love' (1977)
- Chic: 'Le Freak' (1978), 'Good Times' (1979)
- Earth, Wind & Fire: 'September' (1978), 'Boogie Wonderland' (1979)
- K.C. & The Sunshine Band: 'Get Down Tonight' (1975), 'That's The Way (I Like It)' (1975), '(Shake, Shake, Shake) Shake Your Booty' (1976)
- Sister Sledge: 'We Are Family' (1979)
- Gloria Gaynor: 'Never Can Say Goodbye' (1974), 'I Will Survive' (1979)
- George McCrae: 'Rock Your Baby' (1974), 'I Get Lifted' (1975)
- The Jackson 5: 'Dancing Machine' (1973)
- Barry White: 'You're The First, The Last, My Everything' (1974)
- Diana Ross: 'Upside Down', 'I'm Coming Out' (1980)
- The Bee Gees: 'Stayin' Alive' (1977), 'Night Fever' (1978)
- Village People: 'Y.M.C.A.' (1978), 'Go West' (1979)
- Boney M: 'Daddy Cool' (1975), 'Ma Baker' (1977), 'Rasputin' (1978).

Many 1970s and 1980s rock and pop acts were influenced by disco, including The Rolling Stones, David Bowie, ABBA and Rod Stewart.

Technology and production

- Large-scale multitrack recording used for big ensembles; two or more tape machines synced to give extra tracks
- Big, rich sound – lots of **reverb** on vocals and horn parts; deep bass; emphasised high frequency content compared to previous music but not as bright as the recordings of today
- Guitar sound is clean, bright and thin
- Keyboards – Fender Rhodes and Wurlitzer electric pianos; Hohner clavinet; synthesisers
- Use of **wah wah** and **chorus** on guitars and also keyboards
- Early use of **analogue** sequencers and drum machines
- Popularised the use of electronic hand claps
- Deeper kick drum sound by triggering a low synth note to play in time with it
- Songs released as 12" singles running to seven or eight minutes; the song could then run for longer in the clubs
- The idea of the remix originates here – the extended mix, featuring the instrumental, would include new parts such as percussion and keyboards or solos, or would just rework the arrangement by removing parts of the mix
- DJs would beat match and mix the songs together so there was no gap when starting a new song.

Funk

Dates	Late 1960s to early 1980s.
Instrumentation	Similar to disco; vocals were not always used and tended to be more raucous and R&B-influenced than the smooth sound of disco. Some ensembles were smaller, though horn sections were often used.
Influences	■ R&B ■ Soul ■ Jazz (particularly bebop) ■ Psychedelic rock ■ Latin.

Key facts

- The 'authentic' and underground relative of disco, with less commercial success but more respect from musicians and discerning fans

- Performances were exuberant and energetic with lively, chaotic stage shows, with a rebel, anti-establishment image
- The influence of funk continued into the 1980s with artists such as Prince and pop acts like Level 42
- In the 1990s, the UK acid jazz style borrowed heavily from funk and jazz funk in music by Brand New Heavies, Galliano and Jamiroquai.

Main artists

- James Brown: 'Get Up (I Feel Like Being) A Sex Machine' (1970), 'Get Up Offa That Thing' (1976)
- Funkadelic: *One Nation Under A Groove* (1978)
- Isaac Hayes: *Shaft* (1971)
- Sly & The Family Stone: 'Everyday People' (1968), 'Family Affair' (1971)
- Stevie Wonder: 'Living For The City' (1973), 'Sir Duke' (1977), 'I Ain't Gonna Stand For It' (1980).

James Brown was often described as the 'Godfather of Soul', but he considered his music to be R&B, not soul, and was very influential in developing funk. His raw, aggressive, stripped-down sound, his flamboyance as a performer and the discipline with which he ran his band formed the early sounds of funk music.

Other funk bands included The Isley Brothers and Kool & The Gang. You will notice that some of the acts are also categorised as soul. Some disco bands such as Chic and Earth, Wind & Fire can also be considered funk bands.

Technology and production

- Similar to disco, though usually with more focus on the live recording of real musicians and fewer production tricks.

JAZZ-FUNK AND FUNK-ROCK

- 1970s with an influence on 1980s and 1990s rock
- Funk grooves with jazz top lines and harmony/chord structures
- Jazz keyboard player Herbie Hancock's *Head Hunters* (1973) was a landmark album
- Jazz trumpeter Miles Davis experimented with this type of fusion
- Weather Report played jazz-funk as well as jazz-rock fusion
- Stanley Clarke was a virtuoso slap-bass player
- Bands such as Jane's Addiction and Red Hot Chili Peppers used many funk influences in their brand of 1980s and 1990s rock.

Reggae

Dates	Late 1950s to present day.
Instrumentation	Vocals and often three – or four-part backing vocals; drums, bass, percussion, electric guitar (often more than one), piano, organ, synthesisers, horn section.
Influences	■ Blues ■ R&B ■ Gospel ■ Soul.

Key facts

■ From Jamaica, where the music industry started recording local artists in the late 1950s to play on sound systems – mobile rigs with huge speaker stacks and powerful **amplifiers** that play dance music

■ MCs (Master of Ceremonies) would 'toast' the crowd using a microphone, which evolved into the toasting style of lyrical chanting; they were also known as DJs

■ Studio owners would have their own sound – based on a pool of musicians, arrangers and songwriters to record and write for many different singers and vocal groups, like the Motown and Stax approach

■ Studio One, run by Coxsone Dodd and Treasure Isle, owned by Duke Reid, were the two biggest early studios.

Main artists

■ The Skatalites: 'Guns Of Navarone' (1962), 'Man In The Street' (1964)

■ Alton Ellis: 'Get Ready – Rock Steady', 'Cry Tough' (1966)

■ Bob Marley & The Wailers: 'I Shot The Sheriff', 'Get Up, Stand Up' (1973), *Exodus*, 'One Love' (1977)

■ Jimmy Cliff: *Wonderful World, Beautiful People* (1969), *The Harder They Come* (1972), 'Many Rivers To Cross' (1972)

■ Burning Spear: 'Slavery Days' (1975), 'Black Disciples' (1976)

■ Dennis Brown: 'Money In My Pocket' (1977), 'Milk And Honey' (1977)

- Eek-A-Mouse: *Wa-Do-Dem* (1981)
- Gregory Isaacs: *Night Nurse* (1982), 'Rumours' (1988)
- Shabba Ranks: 'Mr. Loverman' (1992)
- Damian Marley: 'Welcome To Jamrock' (2005).

Technology and production

- Heavy bass with plenty of low **frequency** content, heavily compressed and prominent in the mix
- Drums recorded with lots of isolation, and treated with **gates** and **compression** to achieve a separated and punchy sound
- **EQ** used to remove low frequencies from the piano and guitar chops. This makes them sound much thinner, the piano often unnaturally so.
- Organ shuffle usually mixed fairly quietly; sometimes the left-hand part is barely distinguishable
- The sparseness of the playing leaves lots of room for additional guitars and keyboards
- Vocals and horns recorded and mixed with lots of clarity (usually)
- Plenty of **reverb** used to give a sense of space to dry, close-mic recordings.

Ska

- First sound to emerge in the late 1950s and early 1960s. It has off-beat chords played by the **rhythm section**, similar to reggae but at roughly double the tempo
- Featured horn sections playing instrumental tunes, like the swing bands from America
- By the late 1960s, the beat slowed down and went through the brief rock steady period before becoming the reggae style
- Desmond Dekker's 'Israelites' was a UK number one in 1969.

Ska revival

- In the UK, in the late 1970s, there was a new sound that emerged with bands like The Specials, The Beat and Madness
- Playing ska-based tunes, fused with a punk-like energy and approach, the short-lived style nevertheless provided a platform for UK acts like Madness and UB40 to have long careers with much commercial success.

Roots reggae

- Used political, social and Rastafarian themes
- Came to dominate in the 1970s with artists like Burning Spear, Culture, Israel Vibration, Bunny Wailer and Black Uhuru gaining success in Jamaica and abroad.

Dub

- Dub instrumentals, using mainly just drums and bass, were used by sound systems for the DJs to 'toast' on
- Stripped down to drums and bass by muting other tracks on the **mixing desk**
- Snare or sidestick with splashes of large amounts of **reverb** (spring or plate in 1960s and 1970s)
- Dropping instruments, vocals and horns in and out with added tape **delay**, and often many repeats
- Large amounts of reverb to place instruments far in the distance
- Instruments allowed to 'leak' into the reverb send so there is no dry signal, only effected sound – also happens from leak into drum mics
- Phasing or flanging applied to sections of the mix or individual instruments
- **EQ sweeps** – manually changing the **frequency** of a boosted EQ
- Timed delay on snare, piano/guitar chops or the hi-hats
- The engineer 'plays' the studio like an improvised performance.

Dub producers

- King Tubby: *King Tubbys Meets Rockers Uptown* (1976)
- Lee 'Scratch' Perry: *Return Of The Super Ape* (1978)
- Scientist: *Scientist Meets The Space Invaders* (1981).

Dancehall/Ragga

- In the late 1980s, the dancehall or ragga style emerged, using electronic sounds
- Featured more aggressive lyrics, concerned with gangsters and crime compared to the 'conscious' themes of earlier styles.

Reggae continues to the present day, as well as the roots style which re-emerged during the 1990s.

Acoustic and folk

Country

Dates	Early 20th century to present day.
Instrumentation	Acoustic guitar, electric guitar, bass, drums, violin, banjo, pedal steel guitar, harmonica, keyboards, percussion; sometimes strings and horns. Vocals and backing vocals. The use of acoustic instruments is prominent – acoustic guitar playing rhythmic strumming, chops or picking. Some styles are purely acoustic; others use typical rock band instruments together with acoustic instruments.
Influences	■ European folk music (especially British and Irish) ■ Blues.

Key facts

- Southern states of the US; generally played by European-origin settlers
- Lyrics often refer to a rural country lifestyle
- Sub-genres include bluegrass (fast, entirely acoustic music, often instrumental, featuring banjo and violin and Western-swing) taking influence from the popular swing bands in the 1930s and 1940s to play jazz-influenced songs
- The Nashville recording industry is one of the biggest centres anywhere in the world. Many rock bands have recorded there, including The Rolling Stones.

Main artists

- Jimmie Rodgers (early country): 'Blue Yodel' (1927)
- Spade Cooley (Western swing): 'Shame On You' (1945)
- Earl Scruggs (bluegrass banjo picking): 'Foggy Mountain Breakdown' (1969)
- Hank Williams: 'Hey, Good Lookin'' (1951), 'Your Cheatin' Heart' (1953)
- Johnny Cash: 'Folsom Prison Blues' (1955), 'I Walk The Line' (1956), 'Ring Of Fire' (1963)
- Patsy Cline: 'Crazy' (1961)
- Jim Reeves: 'He'll Have To Go' (1960), 'Distant Drums' (1966)
- Tammy Wynette: 'D-I-V-O-R-C-E' (1969), 'Stand By Your Man' (1969)

- Charlie Daniels Band: 'The Devil Went Down To Georgia' (1979)
- Willie Nelson: 'Georgia On My Mind' (1977)
- Dolly Parton: 'Jolene' (1973), 'I Will Always Love You' (1974), 'Heartbreaker' (1978)
- Shania Twain: *Come On Over* (1997).

Technology and production

- The recording industry in Nashville is world-renowned – there are many top studios that have been at the forefront of music production since the 1960s
- Focus is usually on creating clean, clear, accurate recordings of the actual instruments, particularly acoustic ones, rather than lots of production tricks
- Electric guitar sound is often clean and slightly twangy.

American folk-rock and country-rock in the 1960s

Key facts

- The American music charts were dominated by the success of the British Invasion in the early 1960s, as well as the soul sounds emerging from the southern United States
- Rock'n'roll had lost its popularity, and America was looking for its own new sound
- What emerged were the folk-rock and country-rock styles.

Bob Dylan

- Solo: acoustic guitar, vocals and harmonica; later with rock band line-up
- Dylan's music had its origins in folk, featuring a narrative and a focus on story-telling and incorporating poetic lyrics exploring politics and philosophy – message music
- In 1963, 'Blowin' in the Wind' was an early success, with the album *The Freewheelin' Bob Dylan*
- Dylan's songwriting skill was noticed by other bands, with several songs recorded by different artists like The Byrds and The Hollies
- He was closely involved with the American civil rights movement, campaigning for equality, and later against the Vietnam War; his music helped to politicise a large segment of rock culture
- His third album from 1964, *The Times They Are A-Changin'*, contained political songs about the issues of poverty, racism and the need for social change. The title track is one of Dylan's best-known songs

- The influence of The Beatles and other rock acts led to the inclusion of electric guitars and a rock band line-up for Dylan's 1965 album *Bringing It All Back Home*
- Further hits followed including 'Like A Rolling Stone', 'Lay Lady Lay' and 'Knockin' On Heaven's Door'.

Other important folk-rock and country-rock artists include Neil Young, Crosby, Stills & Nash, Joni Mitchell, The Allman Brothers and The Eagles (who wrote 'Hotel California').

Modern folk and acoustic music

Key facts

- Folk music in the 1970s began to be incorporated into other styles as Genesis and Jethro Tull began to folk elements into progressive rock music
- Pentangle and solo singers such as John Martyn continued to play largely traditional folk songs accompanied by guitars and other traditional instruments
- The 1980s saw the emergence of bands such as The Pogues who explored Irish folk with a punk aesthetic
- Capercaillie released their first album in 1984; their music includes some traditional Gaelic songs and some which are more modern and in English
- In the 1990s, there was something of a resurgence in folk-influenced music, with artists such as Kate Rusby, performing more traditional folk music with a modern twist
- In the early 2000s, a number of pop artists recorded acoustic versions of their songs and Radio One's 'Live Lounge' gained popularity
- The loop pedal gave musicians the flexibility to layer parts and build up textures; Ed Sheeran headlined Glastonbury in 2017 using only a guitar and a loop pedal
- Frank Turner's music fuses elements of folk and acoustic music with punk, with some of his songs written about themes associated with England.

Main artists

- Bob Dylan: 'The Times They Are A-Changin'' (1963), 'Like A Rolling Stone' (1965)
- Joni Mitchell: 'Both Sides Now' (1969), 'Big Yellow Taxi' (1970)
- Capercaillie: 'Fear A' Bhàta' (1988), 'Rann Na Mona' (1991) 'Skye Waulking Song' (2000)
- Billy Bragg: 'A New England' (1983), 'Must I Paint You A Picture?' (1988)
- Kate Rusby: 'Bring Me A Boat', *Underneath The Stars* (2003), *Awkward Annie* (2007)

- Seth Lakeman: 'Lady Of The Sea' (2006), 'Race To Be King' (2008)
- Noah and the Whale: *Peaceful, The World Lays Me Down* (2008), '5 Years Time' (2008), *Last Night On Earth* (2011), 'L.I.F.E.G.O.E.S.O.N.' (2011)
- Mumford and Sons: *Sigh No More*, (2009), 'The Cave' (2010), *Babel* (2012), *Wilder Mind* (2015)
- Frank Turner: *Sleep Is For The Week* (2007), *England Keep My Bones* (2011), *Tape Deck Heart* (2013)
- Fleet Foxes: *Fleet Foxes* (2008), *Helplessness Blues* (2011), *Crack-Up* (2017)
- Bon Iver: *For Emma, Forever Ago* (2007*)*, *Bon Iver, Bon Iver* (2011), *22, A Million* (2016)
- Laura Marling: *Alas, I Cannot Swim* (2008), *I Speak Because I Can* (2010), *Semper Femina* (2017)
- Ed Sheeran: 'The A Team' (2011), 'Thinking Out Loud' (2014), 'Shape of You', 'Galway Girl' (2017).

Commercial pop

Key facts

- Although bands had been 'manufactured' as far back as the 1960s (The Monkees and The Sex Pistols, for example), it wasn't until the 1980s that record labels began to take artists and pair them with popular producers to create an entire genre of music aimed at the mass market
- There are a variety of stylistic origins; from R&B to disco and new wave, but the influence of synth pop, combined with these rapid advances in technology, led to a lot of electronic sounds, studio effects, and a tendency for music to be 'over-produced'
- Commercial pop in the 1980s was pioneered by production teams, the most famous of which was Stock Aitken Waterman
- The development of the boy band and girl band was led by commercial pop music and the artist was often judged on looks and how well they could dance as much as their musical ability
- Modern commercial pop songs may have many writers to create the ultimate pop song; *Lemonade* by Beyonce featured 72 writers, and Kanye West's *The Life Of Pablo* boasted over 100
- In recent years, commercial pop has begun to overlap with other genres, particularly R&B, hip-hop and dance music – overlap has always existed with dance music, but this has become more exaggerated in recent years.

STOCK AITKEN WATERMAN

This trio of producers would write, produce and manage the careers of singers, and worked with artists such as Dead or Alive, Bananarama and Kylie Minogue. They dominated the charts, and sometimes featured five or more songs in the top 10 in a given week.

Backing tracks were recorded quickly and cheaply using sequencers. Many songs sounded very similar using the same sounds and production. Songs made heavy use of the Linn 9000 drum machine, and the drummer credit in the sleeve note would often refer to 'A. Linn' as the drummer for the song in question, as an 'in-joke'.

Main artists

- Cliff Richard and The Shadows: See *Rock'n'Roll*, page 81
- Sandie Shaw: '(There's) Always Something There To Remind Me' (1965), 'Puppet On A String' (1967)
- Cilla Black: 'Love Of The Loved' (1963), 'Anyone Who Had A Heart' (1964), 'You're My World' (1964), 'You've Lost That Lovin' Feelin'' (1965), 'Alfie' (1966), 'Step Inside Love' (1968)
- Lulu: 'Shout' (1964), 'Boom Bang-A-Bang' (1967)
- The Dave Clark Five: 'Glad All Over' (1964), 'Catch Us If You Can' (1965)
- Michael Jackson: 'Don't Stop 'Til You Get Enough', 'Rock With You' (1979), *Thriller* (1982), 'Billie Jean', 'Beat It', 'Wanna Be Startin' Something', *Bad* (1987), *Dangerous* (1991)
- Madonna: 'Holiday' (1983), 'Like A Virgin' (1984), 'Material Girl', 'Into The Groove' (1985), 'Papa Don't Preach' (1986), 'Who's That Girl' (1987), 'Like A Prayer' (1989), 'Vogue' (1990) and 'Justify My Love' (1990), *Ray Of Light* (1998)
- Bananarama: 'Cruel Summer' (1984), 'Venus' (1986), 'I Heard A Rumour' (1987)
- Kylie Minogue: 'The Loco-Motion', 'I Should Be So Lucky' (1988), 'Better The Devil You Know' (1990), 'Spinning Around' (2000), 'Can't Get You Out Of My Head' (2001)
- Girls Aloud: 'Sound Of The Underground' (2002), 'Love Machine' (2004), 'Call The Shots' (2007), 'The Promise' (2008)
- Leona Lewis: 'Bleeding Love' (2007), 'Collide' (2011)
- One Direction: *Up All Night,* 'What Makes You Beautiful' (2011), 'Live While We're Young' (2012), 'Best Song Ever' (2013)
- Little Mix: *DNA* (2012), 'Black Magic' (2013), *Glory Days*, 'Power' (2016).

There is simply not the space to go into more detail here, but it is interesting to 'dip into' different top 40 charts from the 1960s to present day to give you an idea about the commercial pop music in the charts at each time. The *AS and A Level Music Technology Study Guide* also goes into more detail.

Urban and hip hop

Dates	Mid to late 1970s.
Instrumentation	Vocals (predominantly male) – rapping; drum machine, record decks (turntables), samplers, synthesisers; sometimes with live instruments like guitar, keyboards, drums, percussion, bass, saxophone and other horns.
Influences	<ul><li>Funk</li><li>Disco</li><li>Soul</li><li>R&B</li><li>Reggae – toasting on sound systems, dub</li><li>Scat singing.</li></ul>

Key facts

- Block parties were part of the culture of the young black population in areas like the New York Bronx, with big speaker stacks and powerful amps used to play loud dance music
- The idea of DJs playing stripped-down instrumental dance records with an MC on a microphone is similar to the toasting used by MCs on reggae sound systems
- Dancers created a style called breakdancing – a combination of gymnastics and dance
- Rap didn't have much commercial success in the early 1980s, though some songs did become international hits; the sound had an influence on

pop music – the way beats were put together, using sampled loops and scratching, was copied by producers

- The early sound became known as old-school rap

- Run-D.M.C. and The Beastie Boys were some of the first acts to gain consistent chart success in the late 1980s and into the 1990s; their sound used drum machines and synths rather than loops taken from records – this was known as the golden age of rap

- Public Enemy and De La Soul's music used lots of samples. Many of their songs were made entirely from samples, but these were often cut up and manipulated beyond recognition. De La Soul's first two albums 3 *Feet High and Rising* and *De La Soul Is Dead* used an Akai S-900, EMU SP-12 and a Casio SK-5. Their virtuosic work with sampling technology, which was in its infancy was very skilled

- Public Enemy was successful from the mid-1980s to the early 1990s; their sound was hard, heavy and thick, with edgy rhythms and delivery of raps, to match the gravity of the messages. As with many hip hop songs, many of their hits had lyrics that dealt with serious issues – the social situation of African-Americans, and political issues

- This evolved into the much more hard-line stance of gangsta rap, which promotes violence against enemies and society in general, and a criminal gang lifestyle

- Women are treated as objects to be bought and sold, and pimping is promoted and glorified

- Acts like N.W.A. were forerunners of this approach, and made West Coast hip hop from Los Angeles a more popular style than the East Coast (New York)

- Dr. Dre and Snoop Dogg were also prominent in the West Coast scene

- Dr. Dre was originally a member of N.W.A., and went on to become one of the foremost producers in hip hop, working with many artists including Eminem

- West Coast hip hop has a smoother, more funk-influenced sound than East Coast hip hop and this helped it achieve more commercial success, which by the early 1990s was becoming widespread and continues currently – rap has been at the forefront of pop-chart success throughout the 2000s

- During the 1990s and early 2000s, the barrier between hip hop and R&B got more blurred as singers would feature on tracks with rappers and vice versa

- Urban music has also had a big influence on commercial modern pop

- There has been an increase in the number of collaborations featuring a rap artist and other vocalists, and it is common for EDM tracks to feature a rapped verse or sung vocal hooks to feature in rap and hip hop.

Main artists

- DJ Kool Herc: influential DJ on the early hip-hop scene, but did not release any music that he produced
- Sugarhill Gang: 'Rapper's Delight' (1979)
- Afrika Bambaataa: 'Planet Rock' (1982), 'Renegades Of Funk' (1983)
- Grandmaster Flash: 'The Message' (1982)
- Run-D.M.C.: 'It's Like That' (1983), 'Hard Times' (1984), 'Walk This Way' (1986)
- LL Cool J: 'I Can't Live Without My Radio' (1985), 'I Need Love' (1987)
- Beastie Boys: '(You Gotta) Fight For Your Right (To Party!)', 'No Sleep Till Brooklyn' (1987)
- Public Enemy: 'Don't Believe The Hype' (1988), 'Black Steel In The Hour Of Chaos' (1989)
- N.W.A.: 'Straight Outta Compton' (1988), 'Express Yourself' (1989), 'Alwayz Into Somethin'' (1991)
- M.C. Hammer: *Please Hammer, Don't Hurt 'Em*, 'U Can't Touch This' (1990)
- Coolio: 'Gangsta's Paradise' (1995)
- Eminem: 'My Name Is' (1999), 'The Real Slim Shady', 'Stan' (featuring Dido) (2000), 'Just Lose It' (2004), *Recovery* (2010)
- Kanye West: *Late Registration* (2005), *808s & Heartbreak* (2008), *My Beautiful Dark Twisted Fantasy* (2010), *The Life Of Pablo* (2016)
- Beyonce: 'Irreplaceable' (2006), 'Halo', 'Sweet Dreams' (2009), 'Run The World (Girls)' (2010), 'Drunk In Love (feat. Jay-Z)' (2013), *Lemonade* (2016)
- Dizzee Rascal: 'Fix Up, Look Sharp' (2003), 'Bonkers', 'Dance Wiv Me' (with Calvin Harris) (2009)
- Craig David (blending R&B with UK Garage, see House and garage on page 122): 'Walking Away', 'Rewind' (2000), 'When The Bassline Drops' (with Big Narstie) (2015), 'Ain't Giving Up (with Sigala) (2016)
- Drake: *Take Care* (2011), 'One Dance', *Views* (2016)
- The Black Eyed Peas: 'Where Is The Love?' (2003), *The E.N.D.*, 'I Gotta Feeling' (2009)
- Rihanna: 'Umbrella' (2007), 'Love The Way You Lie' (feat. Eminem), 'Where Have You Been' (2011), 'Diamonds' (2012)
- Stormzy: 'Know Me From', 'Shut Up' (2015), 'Big For Your Boots' (2017).

Other prominent artists include: Snoop Dogg, Puff Daddy (P. Diddy), Tupac Shakur, Wu-Tang Clan, Jay-Z, Nas, Lil Wayne and The Weeknd.

Technology and production

- Based mainly on repeating rhythmic patterns (loops)
- Original hip hop artists, in the early 1980s, used two or more record decks to play instrumental grooves, often drum and bass breaks, while mixing in other patterns or short hits from other records
- Unusual, unique **timbres** created by DJs using scratch techniques on record decks – this involves manipulating the playback of a record, moving it quickly back and forth, speeding up and slowing down
- Later styles also use samplers to create loops, DJ scratching, and unique sounds created by **reversing**, pitch shifting and filtering
- Special effects from synthesisers/non-pitched sound effects
- Drum machines used instead of or alongside loops created by DJs
- Music often had a lo-fi quality because the samples were taken from old vinyl records. Equally, because of the limited memory in early samplers, the sample rates and bit depths were lowered, giving a grainy sound
- Deep bass frequencies – often from kick drum sounds
- Since 2000, developments in DAW technology and computer power have meant that the gap between a DIY bedroom studio and a more expensive studio is gradually shrinking, and the amount of plug-ins, effects and instruments available is increasing all the time
- One of the most common effects in the genre is the extreme use of pitch correction software on vocals as a creative tool.

GRIME

- Grime has its origins in East London
- Tempos around 140 BPM, with half-time sections like Dubstep
- Drumbeats focusing on complex two-step patterns with short, truncated samples
- Arrangements avoid overcomplexity and too much layering, particularly percussion
- Use of vocal hooks with sample **stuttering** to create rhythmic elements and pitch effects.

Electronic dance music

Dates	Mid-1980s to present day.
Instrumentation	Drum machine or drum and percussion samples, synthesisers, samplers, turntables, vocals.
Influences	<ul><li>Disco</li><li>Reggae and dub</li><li>Hip hop</li><li>Synth pop</li><li>Soul</li><li>Funk</li><li>Jazz.</li></ul>

Key facts

- In the mid-1980s, the Chicago house party scene used disused warehouses for all-night dance events; other USA urban areas were soon following the trend

- This gained European popularity in the late 1980s with raves held in fields and warehouses

- From the late 1980s, many mainstream pop singles were also released as various dance mixes on 12" single and CD. Some dance mixes bore little relation to the original single

- UK house scene closely tied to indie – both shared an underground and DIY ethic to music production and sales, and clubs like The Haçienda in Manchester had DJs playing house music and EDM, as well as live indie bands

- Ministry of Sound in London established itself as a leading club for the new dance sound

- Ibiza clubs were important venues for playing house, trance and the new styles that emerged, together with venues in France, Italy, Germany and Spain

- During the 1990s, electronic music was influential on pop music, with artists like Kylie, Madonna and Pet Shop Boys drawing on house, techno and trip-hop influences

- However, many electronic artists remained outside mainstream chart sales

- Most artists are club DJs as well as music producers, remixing other artists' work in their own style.

Main artists

- Early Chicago/Detroit DJs: Frankie Knuckles, Chip E, Larry Heard and Derrick May
- MARRS: 'Pump Up The Volume' (1987)
- Coldcut: 'Doctorin' The House' (feat. Yazz and The Plastic Population) (1988), 'Find A Way' (feat. Queen Latifah) (1990)
- Bomb the Bass: 'Beat Dis' (1987), 'Megablast/Don't Make Me Wait' (1988)
- S-Express: 'Theme From S-Express' (1988)
- Aphex Twin: *Selected Ambient Works 85-92* (1992)
- The Orb: 'Tripping On Sunshine' (1988), 'Blue Room' (1992)
- The KLF: 'Doctorin' The Tardis' (1988)
- Robert Miles: 'Children' (1996)
- Groove Armada: 'At The River' (1998), 'If Everybody Looked The Same' (1999), 'Superstylin' (2001)
- Basement Jaxx: 'Red Alert' (1999), 'Where's Your Head At' (2001)
- Fatboy Slim: 'Trippin' On Sunshine' (1994), 'The Rockafeller Skank' (1998), 'Praise You' (1999)
- Moby: *Play* (1999)
- The Prodigy: 'Charly' (1991), 'Out Of Space' (1992), 'Voodoo People' (1994), 'Firestarter' (1996), 'Smack My Bitch Up' (1997)
- The Chemical Brothers: 'Setting Sun' (1996), 'It Began in Afrika' (2001), 'Galvanize' (2005)
- Daft Punk: 'Around The World' (1997), 'One More Time', 'Harder Better Faster' (2001), *Random Access Memories* (2013)
- Tiësto: 'Adagio For Strings' (2004)
- David Guetta: 'Memories' (2009), 'Titanium' (2011), 'Bang My Head' (feat. Fetty Wap & Sia) (2014), 'This One's For You (feat. Zara Larsson) (2016)
- Calvin Harris: 'Acceptable In The 80s' (2007), *Ready For The Weekend* (2009), *18 Months* (2012), *Funk Wav Bounces Vol. 1* (2017), 'One Kiss' (feat. Dua Lipa) (2018)
- Fedde Le Grand: 'Put Your Hands Up For Detroit' (2006), 'Let Me Think About It' (with Ida Corr) (2007)
- Skrillex: 'Bangarang' (2011)
- Benga: *Diary Of An Afro Warrior* (2008), 'I Will Never Change' (2012), *Chapter II* (2013)
- Skream: *Skream* (2006), *Outside The Box (2010)*
- Avicii: 'Levels' (2011), 'Wake Me Up' (2013), 'Lonely Together' (feat. Rita Ora) (2017)

- Galantis: 'Runaway (U & I)' (2014), 'Peanut Butter Jelly' (2015), 'No Money' (2016)
- Martin Garrix: 'Animals' (2013), 'Scared To Be Lonely' (feat. Dua Lipa) (2017)
- The Chainsmokers: 'Closer' (2016), 'Something Just Like This' (feat. Coldplay), 'Paris' (2017)
- Swedish House Mafia: 'Save The World' (2012), 'Don't You Worry Child' (2013)
- Major Lazer: 'Lean On' (2015), 'Light It Up' (2016), 'Know No Better' (2017)
- Disclosure: 'Latch' (2012), 'White Noise', *Settle*, 'You & Me' (feat. Eliza Doolittle) (2013).

Technology and production

- Use of computer-based sequencers
- Cheap cost of computer-based systems compared to conventional recording technology made music production accessible to many more people than before
- Drum machines or sampled drums – both loops and single hits
- Synthesisers widely used; different styles use synthesisers in different ways, or have certain signature sounds or playing techniques associated with the style
- **Sampling** used extensively – sampled vocals common, together with treatments such as **stuttering**, gapping and pitch-shift
- Use of compressors and **gates** to create pumping and rhythmic effects
- Samples taken from a wide range of instrumental music, singing and spoken word/broadcast
- Vocals are often heavily processed with pitch correction software, which is used as a creative as opposed to solely a corrective effect
- Effects used in a wide variety of ways – **delays** used for creating new rhythmic elements or adding spatial elements; sounds mangled beyond recognition by extreme processing; long, distant **reverbs** used.

Electronic dance includes many sub-genres such as house, techno, trance, drum & bass, chillout, trip hop and ambient.

House and garage

- The House style had its origins with Frankie Knuckles DJing at the Warehouse Club in Chicago, influenced by R&B
- Roland TR-909 used to fatten the kick drum with sparse overall texture
- Larry Levan was the DJ at the Paradise Garage in New York; influenced by soul music, particularly in vocals
- 'Garage' music moved to the UK and became popular in clubs like Ministry of Sound

- Acid House used the Roland TB-303 and had links to the UK rave scene; venues were dotted around the M25 near London to avoid the authorities
- Since 2010, Garage has come back to the forefront, featuring shuffling, swung beats, and with artists such as Disclosure drawing upon these influences with commercial success.

Trance

- Trance music became commercially successful in the 1990s
- It is characterised by four-to-the-floor kick drum patterns with lengthy snare and kick rolls that build in **velocity** through progressive diminution
- Roland JP-8000 used to create the characteristic 'SuperSaw' sound; a number of **oscillators** creating slightly detuned sawtooth waves
- Rapid synth **arpeggiator** patterns with a central hook or melody, and atmospheric breakdown sections.

Jungle and drum & bass

- Originated in London in the early 1990s
- Amen break – a fast drum pattern sampled from a funk record; breakbeats commonly used
- Tempo tends to be between 160-180BPM with complex syncopated and percussive loops
- Uses Jamaican/Caribbean sound-system production methods and influences from dub reggae, such as toasting
- TR-808 kick is important, with heavy bass and sub-bass.

Chillout, ambient and trip hop

- These styles use down-tempo beats and thinly spaced textures
- The production methods are similar to electronic dance
- Massive Attack (*Mezzanine*, 1998) and Portishead (*Portishead*, 1997) were pioneers of the trip hop style
- London Grammar (*If You Wait*, 2013 and *Truth Is A Beautiful Thing*, 2017) blend ethereal lyrics with ambient textures.

Dubstep

- Originated in South London and supported by John Peel
- Big basslines, reverberant drum lines and clipped samples
- Syncopated and shuffle rhythms with 138-142 BPM tempo and a pronounced clap or snare on beat three; half-time feel
- 'Wub' or 'wobble' bass – **LFO** used to manipulate volume and filter cutoff frequency of the synth bass line, creating a repeated note/**tremolo** effect

- Builds to a 'drop'; the percussion will pause and the instruments will re-enter along with sub-bass and **portamento** synth effects that sometimes drop a full octave.

Music for the media: computer game and film

Music for film

Key facts

- Modern films combine the orchestral textures with electronic instruments, and some films use a solely electronic 'palate' to work from
- With the use of **DAW** software, the composer can sketch their composition to the images and generate a click track to ensure that every point between images and music is perfectly timed.

Main artists

- Carmine Coppola and Francis Ford Coppola: *Apocalypse Now* (1979)
- Vangelis: *Chariots of Fire* (1981), *Blade Runner* (1982, soundtrack released 1994)
- John Williams: *Star Wars* (1977), *Superman* (1978), *E.T.* (1982), *Jurassic Park* (1993)
- James Horner: *Titanic* (1997), *Avatar* (2009)
- Hans Zimmer: *The Dark Knight* (2008), *Inception* (2010)
- Daft Punk: *Tron: Legacy* (2010).

HANS ZIMMER

- When composing the music for *Inception* (2010), Zimmer used a large ensemble made up of a huge brass section, synthesisers and Johnny Marr's electric guitar
- The brass section is unusually large, and Zimmer uses the orchestra to recreate the **pitch bends**, **tremolos** and ambient effects he had previously made using synthesisers.

NOTE: For each film, please check age rating before viewing.

Technology and production

- The **DAW**, samplers and soft synths, have made the film composer's job significantly easier because they allow the composer to try out different musical ideas and synchronise them with the film before committing to final musical ideas and recording them with an orchestra
- Although most film music still relies very heavily on orchestral music, the development of synthesisers has allowed electronic sounds to be used as part of orchestral scores
- Films such as *Blade Runner* used electronic textures imaginatively and the synthesisers were used to create soundscapes, sound effects and otherworldly textures
- The use of high-quality sampled instruments means that it is possible to create music using very realistic sounds on a computer running a DAW.

Music for computer games

Key facts

- One of the early computer games featuring music was Space Invaders (Taito) in 1978. It had a continuous background soundtrack and the musical material was made up of four descending chromatic notes that repeat in a loop to create a bass line
- Game music from the 1980s has gained cult status for its simplicity and has been sampled in other popular music
- The music for *Super Mario* in 1985 was a milestone for Nintendo; it constantly changed and developed to match the action
- *Star Wars* games took music composed by John Williams for the films of the 1970s and 1980s and used it for the game soundtracks
- Computer game music today follows the same artistic intent as that for films, often increasingly composing for large orchestral forces.

Main artists

- Tomohiro Nishikado: *Space Invaders* (1978)
- Nobuo Uematsu: *Final Fantasy* (1987), *Final Fantasy VI* (1994)
- Hirokazu Tanaka: *Tetris Theme* (1989 – arranged)
- Martin O'Donnell and Michael Salvatori: *Halo* (2002)
- Tommy Tallarico and Emmanuel Fratianni: *Advent Rising* (2005)
- Jesper Kyd: *Hitman* (2000), *Assassin's Creed* (2007)
- Jeremy Soule: *The Elder Scrolls V: Skyrim* (2011).

NOTE: For each game, please check the age rating before playing.

Technology and production

- Early arcade game music was usually **monophonic**, looped and used sparsely (as a theme and possibly between levels); they had limited polyphony, and the Nintendo Entertainment System (1983) could only play three notes at once

- Background music would stop while the sound effect played and composers had to be creative in creating the illusion of more notes playing

- In the 1980s, advances in technology meant that some games started to use sampled sounds, and FM synthesis

- By the mid-1980s, FM synthesis was built into computers, allowing greater depth to timbres than the beeps previously used from internal speakers

- Space Invaders (1978) was an early example of a game where the music was interactive and linked to the action in the gameplay – the music sped up as time crept on. This was not the norm until the mid-1980s

- The soundtrack for 'GliderRider' (ZX Spectrum, 1986) was written by David Whittaker, and incorporated different moods of music for motorbiking and hang-gliding

- Interactivity is now used across the majority of computer game music, with the mood changing according to the scenes and the gameplay

- The 8-bit Sega Master system was released in 1986. It featured four dedicated sound channels: three for music and one for **noise**

- Games in the 1990s used CD quality music with realistic instrumental **timbres**; in 1995, Sony released the PlayStation. It used 32-bit technology and the 24-channel sound chip provided CD quality stereo sound with built-in support for digital effects such as **reverb**

- In 2001, the first Xbox was released with Microsoft promising 'movie-like' sound. The specification included a 64-voice audio processor with 64MB of memory and a 200MHz CPU

- Nintendo released the GameCube in the same year. Whilst less of a commercial success, its sound specifications were better than the Xbox, with a dedicated 16-bit DSP powering 64 channels at a 48kHz **sample rate**

- Video game music today is pre-recorded; this provides a number of advantages over sequenced music previously used. The Xbox 360 supports digital stereo PCM audio at 48kHz and the PlayStation 3 can handle sample rates up to 192kHz

- With this advancing technology, computer game music now includes the same breadth and complexity as film music, and this allows composers to have increasing creative freedom.

Exam Guidance

- It's much better to try and keep your answers brief, concise and to the point than to repeat the same thing lots of times
- Bullet points can be a good way of doing this. You can extend and add detail to each point. You can also use subheadings to organise your answers for extended response questions
- Keep your answers as specific as you can. General responses like 'use of effects', 'delay' or 'reverb' probably won't give the examiner enough information
- Concentrate on answering the question asked on the exam paper, not the one you've prepared a perfect answer for!
- However, providing statements such as 'a crotchet delay has been used on the lead vocal', or 'the reverb on the snare drum has a long reverb time' will tell us a lot more about what you are hearing
- Make sure that your handwriting is clear and legible – if the examiner can't read your answer, they can't give it credit
- Look carefully at the number of marks each question carries; for shorter answers, this will be the number of relevant points you need to make
- For extended response questions, your answer will be given an overall level band based on the quality of your response
- There is often more space provided than you need to fully answer the question – don't feel like you have to fill all of the lines! Instead, focus on clearly and concisely answering the question to the best of your ability.

Question types

Gap fill, line matching and multiple-choice questions

- You might have to fill in a missing word in a sentence, or match up information by drawing a line between related words or phrases
- Some questions will give you options from which you have to pick the correct answer; for example, identifying a specific instrument from a list or identifying an effect.

Short answers

- These questions ask you to provide information but you don't have to write it in a complete sentence
- You should make sure you answer the question clearly, use the correct terminology, and beware of using abbreviations or providing two contradictory answers

- If you do this, you are unlikely to score credit for your answer, even if part of it is correct
- The key thing to remember is to answer the question by making the appropriate number of points
- If a question has one mark available, then a single answer will suffice
- However, if the question has two or three marks available, then it will require multiple points to achieve full marks.

Tables and diagrams

- You may have to complete a table and provide device parameters, or write a specific number of points; you might also have to make a point and justify it
- The table may be half-complete for you to provide missing information, or with a series of headings for you to fill in the gaps
- Some questions may involve drawing; for example, you might have to complete a graph of a filter and label the axes
- Diagrams can be used to illustrate your points in longer answer questions; for example, when drawing a filter
- The examiner is looking for you to demonstrate your knowledge of music technology, and will not be judging your artistic ability
- Label your diagram accurately and make it as clear as possible.

Open questions

- There are more possible responses for open questions than short answers, tables or gap fills
- Use bullet points, or perhaps subheadings to keep your answer focused
- Make sure you've looked at the mark allocation for the question; it's important that you have supplied enough detail for you to gain the maximum number of marks
- You may have to provide a point and a justification, so it is important that you expand each of the points you make.

Practical questions

- As part of Component 4, you will have to demonstrate practical skills, and bounce down the resulting audio to be assessed

Find out more about the structure of Component 4 on page 10.

- You may, for example, be asked to remove **noise**, apply an effect or processing to a track or to **synthesise** a sound based on another audio file.

COMMON MISTAKES IN PRACTICAL QUESTIONS

Be especially careful of the following things when completing the practical questions in Component 4:

- **Bouncing just a few bars or a single audio region.** Remember to listen to all your bounces before the end of the exam to check they all play back as you expect them to
- **Leaving the metronome on.** It's important that you switch the metronome off before you bounce the track
- **Soloing/muting a track accidentally for the final mix.** Have a final listen through of your mix and make sure everything plays as it should
- **Not soloing the track you're asked to.** Equally, for the interim bounces, you need to follow the instructions on the paper and solo the track you are asked to
- **The tracks being out of sync.** Make sure you read the instructions for each question and the music starts playing where it should for each individual track
- **Cutting off the reverb tail.** Carefully listen to the end of your bounce to make sure the reverb tail naturally decays. You should follow the specific instructions given in question 5.

All of these errors can be easily avoided – leave yourself sufficient time to carefully listen to your bounces, all the way through, to make sure you haven't made any careless mistakes.

Extended response questions

- You will draw upon your knowledge and understanding of music technology and apply this in order to make a judgement or reach a conclusion
- You may analyse a stimulus (like a picture of a synthesiser or a photo of a microphone placement) and make connections and comparisons between different audio (like discussing the differences in production between two tracks)
- You will demonstrate higher level skills in application, conclusion, analysis, connection and thinking logically
- Structure your answers as you wish, but focus on what the question is asking.

Practice questions

Question 1

Robert Miles – Children

a. When was this track recorded? Put a cross in the correct box. (1)

☒ **A** 1970 – 1979

☒ **B** 1980 – 1989

☒ **C** 1990 – 1999

☒ **D** 2000 – 2009

b. It is unlikely that the repeated synth broken chords heard between 2:27 and 2:40 would be played live. State a way these could be triggered more easily. (1)

c. Fill in the table below to describe two music technology effects or processors that have been used to create the piano sound audible between 0:00 and 0:14. (4)

Effect/Processor	Parameters/Setting
Example: Compression	Example: Low threshold/ high ratio
(1)	(1)
(1)	(1)

d. This track is recorded using synthesisers and drum machines. Fill in the sentences below to identify how the track would be captured and mixed. (2)

Analogue hardware synthesisers have a poorer _____ ratio than DAW plug-ins.

Electronic instruments like synthesisers and drum machines have a narrower _____ range than live instruments.

e. Describe how filtering is used to maintain interest in the mix between 0:28 and 0:38. (2)

_____

_____

(Total for Question 1 = 10 marks)

Question 2

Route 94 (feat. Jess Glynne) – My Love

a. Fill in the missing words in the sentences below to describe the
filtering used in this track.   **(3)**

There is a _____ pass filter used on the lead vocals at the
beginning of the track.

Between 0:00 and 0:31, the _____ frequency gradually _____,
and the filter is removed.

b. Describe the delay effect used on the vocal part on the lyric
'close to me', which happens first between 1:06 and 1:11.   **(4)**

_____

_____

_____

_____

c. This song was recorded on a DAW. Describe **three** benefits of recording
and working with a DAW compared to digital multitrack tape.   **(3)**

1. _____

2. _____

3. _____

(Total for Question 2 = 10 marks)

Question 1:
Robert Miles – Children

a. *C 1990-1999* [1]

b. *Arpeggiator/sequencer* [1]

c. *One mark for each:*

- **Reverb (1)**
  Long decay time (1)
  High wet signal/send amount (1)

- **Delay (1)**
  Crotchet synced delay time (1)
  7+ repeats/High level of feedback (1)
  N.B. Feedback is not on the AS Level Specification
  but this is a valid answer and would be credited.
  Wet signal approx. 50%/medium (1)
  Wet signal panned L (1)

- **EQ (1)**
  High shelf/HF boost (1) [4]

d. *Signal-to-noise (1), Dynamic (1)* [2]

e. *Low pass filter (1),*
Decreasing (1) cutoff frequency (1)
Starts bright/gets more muffled (1) [2]

Question 2:
Route 94 (feat. Jess Glynne) – My Love

a. *Low (1)*
Cutoff (1)
Rises/increases (1) [3]

b. *Alternate panned (1)*
Dry signal central, repeats left then right (1)
Minim delay time/synced (1)
5+ audible repeats/high feedback/send amount (1)
N.B. Feedback is not on the AS Level Specification
but this is a valid answer and would be credited.
Wet signal is quieter than the dry signal (1) [4]

c. *Unlimited tracks (1)*
Ease of access to plug-ins/presets/multiple instances (1)
Use of internet to share projects/transfer of files and recordings (1) [3]

The extended response question

Answering extended response questions

- It is useful for us to think briefly about assessment objectives (AOs)
- In the mark schemes for longer answer questions, you will be shown a split of marks for AO3 and AO4

AO3	Demonstrate and apply knowledge and understanding of music technology
AO4	Use analytical and appraising skills to make evaluative and critical judgements about the use of music technology

- You will need to demonstrate these skills to score highly on the extended response questions for Component 3 and Component 4
- The easiest way to think of it is that AO3 marks are awarded when you demonstrate your knowledge and understanding of music technology
- To achieve AO4 marks, you need to apply this knowledge, evaluating the effectiveness of something (an audio track, a picture or a diagram), or making links between something and other relevant material (perhaps when identifying the wider context to do with the production of a track)
- It's not possible to access AO4 without using AO3 to get there (because as part of AO4, you already have to show your knowledge and understanding)

Compare (Component 3, Question 5)	Evaluate (Component 4, Question 5)
- Make points about the similarities and differences - Make relative judgements	- Make judgements against parameters - Draw conclusions - Justify your opinions or make comparisons

- The final mark awarded for extended response questions is based on an 'overall impression' of the answer. To get an idea of how this works, read the comments on the model answers in this chapter.

Have a go

- Listen to the two tracks in the practice question for Component 3, Question 5 below
- Based on the marks available, it makes sense to spend about 20 minutes on this question in the exam
- Don't look at the mark scheme yet!
- When you've done your best, check what you've written against the indicative content
- Remember – it's only indicative content, and you're not expected to provide all of the information in the mark scheme
- Equally, you might give information that isn't listed on the mark scheme but, as long as it's correct, the examiner will give it credit.

5. **The Smiths: 'Stop Me (If You Think You've Heard This One Before)'**
   Mark Ronson feat. Daniel Merriweather: 'Stop Me'

   Compare the production techniques used in both versions.

Mark scheme

AO3 (8 marks)/AO4 (8 marks)

MARKING INSTRUCTIONS

Markers must apply the descriptors in line with the general marking guidance and the qualities outlined in the levels-based mark scheme below.

Responses that demonstrate **only** AO3 without any AO4 should be awarded marks as follows:

- Level 1 AO3 performance: 1–2 marks
- Level 2 AO3 performance: 3–4 marks
- Level 3 AO3 performance: 5–6 marks
- Level 4 AO3 performance: 7–8 marks

Indicative content guidance

The indicative content below is not prescriptive and candidates are not required to include all of it. Other relevant material not suggested below must also be credited. Relevant points may include:

AO3

Capture – The Smiths

- Multitrack recording
- Bright/lots of high frequencies
- **Tape saturation**

Capture – Mark Ronson

- **DAW**/digital equipment
- Little hiss
- More low frequencies/frequencies more balanced
- More channels available

Instrumentation – The Smiths

- Guitar-based with acoustic/electric/bass guitars
- Acoustic drum kit and vocals
- No **sampling** – all instruments are recorded live

Instrumentation – Mark Ronson

- More instrumental layers with vocals/backing vocals
- Lots of acoustic instruments/use of sampling to create very realistic sounds
- Electronic drum beat/samples/**MIDI**/looped percussion

Dynamics – The Smiths/Mark Ronson

- Both use **compression**
- Mark Ronson version has a narrower dynamic range
- Vocal is heavily compressed on The Smiths version as it's performed relatively quietly
- Both tracks end by fading out

FX – The Smiths

- 'Jangly' electric guitar sound – lightly distorted, with **delay** and **chorus**
- Wide stereo image
- Subtle **reverb** across the mix

FX – Mark Ronson

- Delay on lead vocals
- Vocals lacking in low frequencies/emphasising high mids

AO4

- The overall dynamic range in the Mark Ronson version is narrower than that of The Smiths; this was increasingly common in the late 1990s and 2000s/'loudness wars'. The heavy **compression** applied to the parts and master give a consistent level. This is more common in modern recordings

- The Mark Ronson version combines acoustic and electronic instruments and the acoustic instruments would need more compression due to their wider dynamic range. Equally, The Smiths version uses acoustic guitars, drums and vocals with a range of electric guitars so the same could be observed

- In both versions, the **stereo field** is used extensively to create balance; in The Smiths' version, the different acoustic and electric guitar parts are panned left and right, along with the drum kit overheads and percussion parts (e.g. tambourine panned hard right) to give a wide stereo image. The percussion parts are similarly panned in the Mark Ronson version

- The guitar parts on The Smiths version are made up of lots of overdubs with interlocking riffs and countermelodies. The guitar parts are separated with **EQ**, **panning** and different levels of **distortion**

- The guitar parts on The Smiths version form the main chordal backing, whereas on the Mark Ronson version, this is provided by the **sustained** string chords and bass guitar part with additional interest from the horn section

- The **delay** on the lead vocal in the Mark Ronson version is filtered to remove high frequencies/**low pass filter**

- The Smiths is bass-light compared to the Mark Ronson version. The upper mids and high frequencies are more prevalent. In the Mark Ronson version, the mix is low and high **frequency** heavy. This is demonstrative of the mixing trends of the time; generally, mixes in the 1980s were bright and had more upper mids and high frequencies, whereas more modern masters are low and high frequency heavy

- The guitar solo in The Smiths uses distortion/**overdrive** and its EQ emphasises upper mids/high frequencies to cut through the mix

- There are no backing vocals in The Smiths version. The Mark Ronson version uses overdubbed harmonies that are sung by the same singer, with backing vocal oohs at the start

- The different layers of countermelodies and riffs in the Mark Ronson version would have been a challenge to mix and maintain focus on the vocal; this is achieved through filtering and panning, and by ensuring they sit further back in the mix

- The 'jangly' guitar sound was characteristic of 1980s Indie Rock – lightly distorted, with **chorus** and delay. This occurs throughout The Smiths version. There is a thin-sounding clean electric guitar at the start of Mark Ronson's version, and a lightly distorted guitar playing accompanying chords at various points throughout.

Levels based assessment grid

Level	Mark	Descriptor
	0	**No rewardable material**
Level 1	**1-4**	■ Demonstrates and applies limited knowledge and understanding of production techniques used, some of which may be inaccurate or irrelevant (AO3) ■ Gives limited analysis and deconstruction of production techniques used, making limited comparisons between the two recordings and/or little attempt at chains of reasoning (AO4).
Level 2	**5-8**	■ Demonstrates and applies some knowledge and understanding of production techniques used, which is occasionally relevant but may include some inaccuracies (AO3) ■ Gives some analysis and deconstruction of production techniques used, making some comparisons between the two recordings and/or simplistic chains of reasoning (AO4).
Level 3	**9-12**	■ Demonstrates and applies clear knowledge and understanding of production techniques used, which is mostly relevant and accurate (AO3) ■ Gives clear analysis and deconstruction of production techniques used, making clear comparisons between the two recordings and competent chains of reasoning (AO4).
Level 4	**13-16**	■ Demonstrates and applies detailed knowledge and understanding of production techniques used, which is relevant and accurate throughout (AO3) ■ Gives detailed and accurate analysis and deconstruction of production techniques used, making detailed comparisons between the two recordings and logical chains of reasoning (AO4).

Component 4 – Extended response question

The picture shows an **audio interface** selected by a student to record an acoustic guitar. Evaluate the suitability of the interface to achieve the task.

[16]

Rear

Front

Example answers

Below are two essays that answer the Component 4 that is printed above. Use these as a comparison to help your own essay writing style.

- Have a go at answering the question yourself
- Read the essay by Candidate A below, and compare it to your own work, and the levels based assessment grid
- Compare the essay to the indicative content. Where could the candidates have added more detail, and where have they done well?
- Repeat the process for Candidate B
- Read through the examiners' comments on each answer, and consider where you think your own answer fits
- Make a list of the points you need to remember when answering this question in your real exam.

Candidate A:

You would record an acoustic guitar by placing a microphone around 30cm from the 12th fret of the guitar. This gives an even and balanced sound to the recording, and avoids there being too much rumble, or the sound being too focused on the fretboard.

Phantom power is switched on for a condenser microphone.

The headphone socket would allow the guitarist to hear themselves and monitor their signal to make sure there is no distortion. If the signal was too loud, they could use the 'sens' knob to fix this.

There are jack outputs on the back of the interface and phantom power, which would provide power for the microphone.

It uses a Firewire connection; you don't always get a Firewire socket on a computer so this might be an issue.

Examiner comments:

This answer has some promise and makes an attempt at answering the question. The student begins by discussing acoustic guitar recording, and whilst the points made are valid, they do not completely answer the question. It is important to link the points being made to the interface itself and specifically, how the interface can enable the engineer to do what the student has described. For example – what features of the inputs on the interface are suitable to record a guitar? There are occasions where relevant points are made, but these are not normally linked to the interface.

There is some criticality, as shown by the point about FireWire, but this is limited. The answer is not 'clear' or 'detailed' as the candidate hasn't always fully explained each of their points. They would be well advised to make sure that all points are specifically related to the question, and the stimulus provided for evaluation.

If we look at the levels-based mark scheme and look through the different descriptors, the one that best fits is level 2.

Candidate B:

- The combi inputs on the front of the interface can accept XLR or jack connections. You would be best to use an XLR cable to record the guitar as this is balanced and protects against some interference and noise

- On the back of the interface, phantom power is switched on. This would be appropriate for recording acoustic guitar as you would likely use a condenser microphone. Condenser microphones are a good choice for acoustic guitar recording because they have a flat frequency response, capture the brightness of the guitar and are sensitive

- The 'sensitivity' control is the gain. This is set at its lowest setting for both channels. Because the acoustic guitar is quite a quiet instrument, it likely would need to be higher to get a good signal-to-noise ratio. Otherwise, too much hiss would be recorded and it would be difficult to remove this when processing

- The 'phones' socket allows the musician to hear the click track and record in time with the other tracks previously completed

- 'Mix' would avoid latency issues when the guitarist is recording. If the part is a rhythm guitar, it would be important that the 'groove' of the recording is maintained, and latency would mean that the guitarist might play a little out of time. It would mix some of the direct signal with some of the signal from the computer, and is set at 50% in the photo to provide some of each

- In the picture, the sample rate is set at 192kHz. This will provide a very high-quality recording of the guitar, but will use up more space than necessary on the computer. 44.1kHz would be enough to record the guitar as this is CD quality

- There are balanced jack connectors on the back for monitor speakers; this is a better way of the engineer monitoring the sound of the recording than headphones. Balanced connections avoid interference

- Because there are two inputs, you could use two microphones and record the guitar using a stereo microphone technique, like an XY pair.

Examiner comments:

The answer is well structured and stays 'on track' throughout. Using clear, concise bullet points, the student has discussed many individual controls on the interface and related each one to its impact on acoustic guitar recording. Every bullet point the student makes answers the question, and demonstrates their detailed knowledge and understanding.

The points they make are relevant and accurate and logical, and clearly relate to what the question is asking. The points also explain how you would produce an effective recording of an acoustic guitar. There are evaluative points in this answer; the student identifies that the sample rate is possibly too high and explains why, supported by the information to justify this.

The final point the student makes even goes beyond the AS Level specification; knowledge of stereo microphone techniques is an A Level point. Remember that the mark scheme only shows indicative content, and you could quite possibly make points that are valid but not in the mark scheme. The examiner will still give these credit.

This is a very good answer. If we look at the levels-based mark scheme and look through the different descriptors, the one that fits this answer best is level 4.

Mark scheme

AO3 (4 marks)/AO4 (12 marks)

MARKING INSTRUCTIONS

Markers must apply the descriptors in line with the general marking guidance and the qualities outlined in the levels-based mark scheme below.

Responses that demonstrate **only** AO3 without any AO4 should be awarded marks as follows:

- Level 1 AO3 performance: 1–2 marks
- Level 2 AO3 performance: 3–4 marks
- Level 3 AO3 performance: 5–6 marks
- Level 4 AO3 performance: 7–8 marks

Indicative content guidance

The indicative content below is not prescriptive and candidates are not required to include all of it. Other relevant material not suggested below must also be credited.

Relevant points may include:

AO3

- There are two channels on the interface
- The interface can handle **phantom power** so you could use a **condenser microphone(s)**
- The sensitivity is the gain control
- The **sample rate** will be high enough for a high-quality recording as there are options from 44.1kHz to 192kHz
- FireWire will give a fast connection but there might be compatibility issues, particularly with PCs and more modern Macs.

AO4

- Phantom power is switched on which implies that condenser microphones are being used. Condenser microphones are an appropriate choice due to their sensitivity for quiet acoustic guitars, and wide/flat **frequency** response to capture the brightness of the acoustic guitar
- Sensitivity would be used to set an appropriate gain. It is important to set a gain that gives a good **signal-to-noise ratio** but not one that distorts. Condenser microphones have a higher output volume than dynamics so it is likely that you would not have to turn the sensitivity up too far. This might also depend on the song being played and the playing style
- The sensitivity should be set to maximise the signal-to-noise ratio; recording the guitar too quiet would likely record hiss and this would be detrimental to the quality of the recording and not easy to remove without affecting other important frequencies in the recording
- There is a **limiter** on the back of the guitar that would give some protection against **distortion**. The peak/limit light would illuminate when the limiter is active and when distortion is occurring. You would monitor this as an engineer and ask the guitar player to replay the section if distortion occurred
- The mix control would allow you to avoid issues associated with **monitoring** through the computer. This would improve the quality of the performance as the guitar player would be able to play in time and hear the signal without it having to go in and out of the **DAW**. It is currently set at 50% for both, meaning you would hear a mix of the direct signal and the signal from the computer

- The **sample rate** would likely be set at 44.1kHz as this is CD quality; 192kHz would take up much more disk space and the limitations of both human hearing and your audio equipment means that you would likely hear no difference

- The 1/4" TRS jack connectors on the back of the interface would allow you to listen to the recorded part on monitors. The signal is balanced so provides some protection against interference

- There are extra 1/4" TRS connectors that could be used to supply a separate monitor mix to the guitar player, perhaps with loud drums or clear vocals, or with a click track playing to help with timing

- The interface can be recorded at 24 bit, which is higher than CD quality and gives a greater dynamic range

- 24 bit recording would also give a better signal-to-noise ratio, but realistically, the signal-to-noise ratio of your microphone and studio equipment is likely to be worse than 24 bit so it is unlikely that there would be much benefit in doing so.

Levels based assessment grid

Level	Mark	Descriptor
	0	**No rewardable material**
Level 1	**1-4**	■ Demonstrates limited knowledge and understanding of production techniques/technology used, some of which may be inaccurate or irrelevant (AO3) ■ Shows limited analysis and deconstruction of production techniques/technology used with unsuccessful attempts at chains of reasoning (AO4) ■ Makes limited evaluative and/or critical judgements about the production techniques/technology used (AO4) ■ Makes an unsupported or generic conclusion, drawn from an argument that is unbalanced or lacks coherence (AO4).

Level 2	5-8	■ Demonstrates knowledge and understanding of production techniques/technology used, which are occasionally relevant but may include some inaccuracies (AO3) ■ Shows some analysis and deconstruction of production techniques/technology used with simplistic chains of reasoning (AO4) ■ Makes some evaluative and/or critical judgements about the production techniques/technology used (AO4) ■ Comes to a conclusion partially supported by an unbalanced argument with limited coherence (AO4).
Level 3	9-12	■ Demonstrates clear knowledge and understanding of production techniques/technology used, which are mostly relevant and accurate (AO3) ■ Shows clear analysis and deconstruction of production techniques/technology used with competent chains of reasoning (AO4) ■ Makes clear evaluative and critical judgements about the production techniques/technology used (AO4) ■ Comes to a conclusion generally supported by an argument that may be unbalanced or partially coherent (AO4).
Level 4	13-16	■ Demonstrates detailed knowledge and understanding of production techniques/ technology used, which are relevant and accurate (AO3) ■ Shows detailed and accurate analysis and deconstruction of production techniques/ technology used, with logical chains of reasoning on occasion (AO4) ■ Makes detailed and valid evaluative and critical judgements about the production techniques/ technology used (AO4) ■ Comes to a conclusion, largely supported by a balanced argument (AO4).

Glossary

ADSR. Attack, Decay, Sustain, Release – the controls on an envelope generator that are used to shape a sound.

Aliasing. Artefacts created when a frequency has not been correctly recreated by an A/D convertor and back to a D/A convertor.

Ambience. The amount of reverb that sound contains either naturally from a room or artificially added by an effect.

Amplifier. A piece of equipment used to boost a signal.

Amplitude. The height of a waveform measured from its mean or zero position to its maximum displacement.

Analogue. When a signal or equipment uses a continuously variable physical quantity.

Arpeggiator. A device that automatically plays the individual notes of a chord as an arpeggio/broken chord.

Artefacts. Unwanted sounds created as a by-product during audio processing.

Attack (dynamics). The length of time it takes once the threshold is crossed for the processor to apply its process, for example when the signal goes above the threshold on a compressor, the attack is the amount of time taken to reduce the signal by the amount specified in the ratio.

Attack (synthesis). The length of time it takes between a note being started and the point at which it reaches its peak.

Audio interface. A device that connects a computer to audio peripherals such as microphones, speakers and musical instruments.

Automation. Programming adjustable parameters to operate automatically during playback and mixing.

Auto-Tune. The trade name for a famous piece of software that automatically changes the pitch to the nearest absolute pitch. Can also be used as a creative effect. Alternatives include Melodyne, FlexPitch, VariAudio.

Aux/Bus. An additional output channel for routing to effects, monitors or as an alternative output. Can be used as a method of grouping channels. Often the same as a bus channel.

Balanced. A connection that has two signals in inversion to one another to reduce noise when put back into phase.

Band pass filter. A combination of an LPF and an HPF, where any frequencies outside the scope of the LPF and HPF pass unaffected.

Bit depth. The number of bits used in each sample in analogue to digital conversion.

Bit rate. The number of bits of data are processed every second.

Capacitance. The storage of an electrical charge in a capacitor.

Capsule. The element of a microphone that responds to the sound vibrations.

Capture. The initial stage of recording in which the sounds are input to the recording device.

Cardioid. The pattern by which some microphones capture sound. Cardioid is roughly heart shaped and picks up sound from the front and sides.

Chorus. A modulation effect that simulates multiple instruments or voices performing simultaneously by duplicating an audio signal. This creates a 'shimmering' or 'thickening' effect. One copy of the signal is slightly delayed and is also slightly detuned using an LFO. The wet and dry signals are then recombined.

Clipping. Overloading a signal so that the top of the waveform becomes squared and causes distortion.

Coarse-tuning. The control on a synthesiser or sampler that moves the tuning of a note in semitones.

Colouration. The effect that equipment can have on the tonal characteristics of audio through its physical design and manufacture.

Combo. A combo is a small jazz ensemble which features 'top line' instruments and a rhythm section. Combos often feature the saxophone, trumpet, trombone and clarinet as 'top-line' instruments and drums, double bass and piano as guitar.

Compression (dynamics). A process for controlling the dynamic range of a sound. It reduces the volume of the peaks of sound above a threshold by a pre-determined ratio.

Condenser microphone. A microphone that captures sound by measuring the changes in capacitance as the diaphragm moves.

Control voltage (CV). A variable voltage signal that is used to control behaviours ranging from the pitch of oscillators to the cutoff setting of filters and more.

Crossfade. A crossfade creates a smooth transition between audio files by fading one out whilst the other fades in.

DAW. Digital Audio Workstation. A piece of software for recording, editing and mixing audio and MIDI files.

Decay. The amount of time that it takes from the peak to drop down to the 'Sustain' level.

Decibels (dB). The unit used to measure sound pressure level. This relates to what we perceive as 'loudness' or 'volume'. Decibels are measured on a logarithmic scale.

De-esser. The process of removing overly emphasised sibilant sounds (including 'S' and 'Sh' sounds) by applying a dynamics processor to certain frequencies.

Delay. The process of delaying a sound electronically and then playing it back after a fixed period of time. Normally blended with the original signal to create an echo effect.

Diaphragm. A small flexible piece of material in a microphone that responds to physical vibrations of sounds which is then converted into an electrical signal.

Digital Signal Processing (DSP). The use of digital processing to apply effects and post-production techniques to a recording or mix within the computer.

Direct injection (DI). A unit that converts high-impedance unbalanced signals (line/instrument level) into low-impedance balanced signals (microphone level).

Distortion. The unwanted sound created when an audio signal overloads and clips, or it can be wanted distortion such as overdrive on an electric guitar.

Dynamic microphone. A microphone that has a moving coil attached to the diaphragm within a magnetic field that generates a small electrical signal.

Dynamics processing. The control of dynamics either manually, or with automated devices such as gates and compressors.

Envelope generators. A synthesiser element that creates the way a sound changes over time by changing a sound's attack, decay, sustain and release.

Equalisation (EQ). The balancing of the amplitude of different frequencies within a sound to alter the treble, mid and bass.

Expander. A process for controlling the dynamic range of a sound. Expanders increase the dynamic range by making quiet sounds even quieter; they do this by reducing the volume of anything that is below a set threshold level.

Fine-tuning. The control on an electronic instrument that adjusts the smaller levels of tuning between fixed notes. Usually measured in cents (100 cents in a semitone).

Flanger. A modulation based effect that is created by altering the phase relationship between two signals by modulating a short delay. Flanging creates a distinctive tone caused by comb-filtering.

Frequency. The pitch of a sound or the number of times a wave repeats in a second. Measured in hertz (Hz) or kilohertz (kHz).

Gain level. The amount of boost applied to the preamp stage of an audio channel. Used either to boost signals to an operable level or to boost beyond that point to drive a signal into distortion for musical purposes.

Gate. A process for controlling the dynamics of a sound. Gates silence a signal once it drops below a threshold to remove noise.

Glide. Control on a synthesiser used to make one note slide smoothly into another if played one after another.

High pass filter. A type of filter that removes only bass frequencies below a set point (cutoff frequency) and allows high frequencies through unaffected.

Jack leads. A common connector used for audio. Can be used for mono, stereo, balanced and unbalanced audio signals. Comes in a range of sizes for different purposes.

Limiter. A process for controlling the dynamic range of a sound. It prevents the peaks of sound going above a pre-defined threshold.

Line level. An audio signal that has a higher level than microphone or instrument level and requires less amplification at the preamp stage.

Looping. An audio or MIDI file of any length that repeats multiple times.

Low Frequency Oscillator (LFO). A signal that oscillates below audible frequencies and found on a synthesiser and modulation based effects. Commonly used to modulate other elements of the sound.

Low pass filter. A type of filter that removes only treble frequencies above a set point (cutoff frequency) and allows low frequencies through unaffected.

Mastering. The final stage of production before music is released. Used to ensure that all tracks are of a similar volume and have appropriate processing applied to them.

MIDI. Musical Instrument Digital Interface. A universal language that is used by musical technology equipment and is used to send instrument and controller information.

Mixing desk. A device for changing the relative levels, affecting the EQ and changing the dynamics of a number of audio signals and blending them together.

Modulation. Literally means 'changing' but normally used to include effects with some movement to them such as chorus, flanger or an LFO.

Monitoring. The equipment used to listen to audio during recording or mixing: speakers or headphones.

Mono. A single sound source, speaker or channel.

Monophonic. A synthesiser that can only play one note at a time.

Multisampling. Several samples of a single sound source, usually at different pitches and velocities, to increase the realism of a sampled instrument.

Multitracking. Recording multiple audio tracks separately and then blending them after recording rather than mixing the channels prior to recording.

Nodes (1). When data points cross.

Nodes (2). The zero crossing of a wave, the point with the minimum displacement.

Noise. Unwanted sound.

Normalising. The boosting of audio by the same amount so that the relative volumes remain the same. Commonly used to boost to the peak volume to the maximum level before distortion (0dB).

Oscillators. A device found in a synthesiser that generates waveforms used for sound generation and modulation.

Overdrive. A form of distortion when waveforms are deliberately clipped for artistic reasons.

Overdubbing. The process of recording additional parts into a recording. Not to be confused with 'takes'.

Pad. A switch on equipment that attenuates the gain by a set amount to prevent clipping.

Panning. Placing a sound within the stereo field (left or right).

Phantom power. 48V provided by a mixing desk or an audio interface to provide power for condenser microphones and DI boxes.

Phase inversion. A control to invert a waveform to counteract the effects of phase cancellation.

Phaser. Effect that modulates an audio signal in-and-out of phase to create an aurally pleasing effect of certain frequencies being amplified and reduced.

Pickup. A device that converts vibrations (magnetic, physical etc.) into an electrical signal for amplification and processing.

Pitch bend. A control on synthesisers to bend the pitch of a note up and down by a predetermined amount.

Pitch-mapping. Samples that have been mapped across the MIDI keyboard by changing the pitch and length of a sample so that it can be played as a musical instrument. Often used in conjunction with multisampling and velocity layering.

Plosive. A sound which results from letters such as 'P', 'D' and 'B', which when spoken directly into a microphone can result in a low frequency 'pop' sound due to the strong air movement on a microphone's diaphragm.

Plug-in virtual instruments. Software musical instruments used either standalone or within a DAW.

Polyphonic. A synthesiser that can play more than one note simultaneously.

Pop shield. A device for reducing plosive sounds when recording with a microphone. Placed between the performer and the microphone.

Portamento. A control on synthesisers to continuously alter the pitch of a note by sliding between the original pitch and the destination pitch.

Proximity effect. The change in bass response captured by a directional microphone depending on the distance of a sound source from the microphone.

Quantise. The rounding of data. Commonly used to fix the timing of rhythms.

Ratio. Commonly found on dynamics processors; the input volume compared to the output volume.

Release (dynamics). The amount of time it takes once the signal falls below the threshold for the processor to stop functioning, for example on a gate when the signal falls below the threshold, the release is the amount of time it takes for the gate to close.

Release (synthesis). The length of time that the note continues after it has stopped being played until it dies away to nothing.

Reverberation (reverb). The ambience found within a sound. Either an acoustic space or an artificially created effect.

Reversing. Playing a piece of audio backwards. On a DAW, this is achieved digitally. With analogue technology, a tape was played backwards to create a reversed effect.

Rhythm section. The section of a band accompanying the melody. Commonly includes a piano, guitar, bass guitar and drums.

Sample rate. The frequency with which a sample of analogue information is taken for conversion into a digital signal. Measured in kHz.

Sampling (1). The conversion of analogue information into digital data.

Sampling (2). Using pre-recorded audio as the stimulus for new musical ideas.

Sequencing. Programming note and velocity information to control an electronic instrument.

Shock mount. A device that suspends a microphone while on a stand to reduce noise from vibrations and other physical movements.

Sidechain. An input that allows the processing to be triggered by an external source. Commonly found on dynamic processors and other effects.

Signal chain. The order in which processing occurs.

Signal-to-noise ratio. The difference between the audio that is being captured and the noise captured simultaneously.

Sound pressure level (SPL). A measurement of the sound level against a reference level; measured in decibels and representing how loud we perceive the sound to be.

Spill. Signal that is captured in a microphone unintentionally, usually from another sound source being captured simultaneously.

Stereo field. Placing audio in a mix so they are perceived by the listener as either being central, left or right.

Streaming. Listening to music or watching video in 'real time'.

Stuttering. When audio (normally a sample) is triggered repeatedly and quickly to make the audio sound like a stutter.

Subtractive (synthesis). Using filters and envelope generators to remove elements of a signal and shape the sound.

Sustain. Most commonly the volume at which the note is held until the key is released, but the sustain level can also refer to parameters such as cutoff frequency or pulse width.

Sweep. Moving a parameter quickly through a wide range of values. Commonly used on the filter cut-off on a synthesiser, or the centre frequency of a band pass filter for a wah wah effect.

Swung rhythm. Two-note rhythms that have an uneven feel. The first note will be longer and heavily accented while the latter note will be shorter and weaker.

Synthesis. Electronically creating musical sounds using oscillators and filters etc.

Tape saturation. The effect of the aurally pleasing soft-clipping caused by recording a signal to an analogue tape that is slightly overloaded.

Threshold. The volume at which dynamics processors begin to operate – once the sound goes above or below the threshold, depending on the processor type, the processing will be applied.

Timbre. A sound's timbre ('tone colour' or 'tone quality') is given by its harmonic content. Different wave shapes will have different harmonic content, and it is possible to make alterations to the timbre of a sound through processes such as filtering.

Transducer. A device that converts between different types of energy, for example, a microphone's capsule converts a sound into electrical energy.

Transistor. An electrical semiconductor that is used for switching or amplification.

Tremolo. An effect that is created by the modulation of volume.

Unbalanced. A cable that only has the signal cable and the connection to ground, e.g. an electric guitar cable.

Valves. A component found in electronic musical equipment for amplification and switching.

Velocity. How hard a note has been struck.

Vibrato. An effect that is created by the modulation of pitch.

Wah wah. An effect that is created by the modulation of a band pass filter to adjust the amount of treble/bass within a sound. Commonly adjusted with a foot controller.

Waveform. The visual representation of audio.

XLR. A connector commonly found on microphones and other balanced signals. Sometimes known as a 'cannon' connector.

Zero crossing. The point at which a waveform has a displacement of 0. You can avoid a click whilst editing if you cut the waveform at this point.

Picture credits:
All drawn diagrams courtesy of Phil Gambrill, page 30: Sibelius inserts courtesy of Imogen Willis, page 139: audio interface images courtesy of James Reevell